# MURDER
## *at Asheville's*
## BATTERY PARK HOTEL

*The Search for Helen Clevenger's Killer*

## ANNE CHESKY SMITH

THE
History
PRESS

Published by The History Press
Charleston, SC
www.historypress.com

*Author photograph courtesy of Nathan Rivers Chesky Photography.*

First published 2021

Manufactured in the United States

ISBN 9781467145602

Library of Congress Control Number: 2021937193

*Notice*: The information in this book is true and complete to the best of our knowledge. It is offered without guarantee on the part of the author or The History Press. The author and The History Press disclaim all liability in connection with the use of this book.

# CONTENTS

# 1

# WHAT A RITZY PLACE... BATTERY PARK HOTEL

Helen Clevenger stepped out of the passenger seat of her uncle's car into familiar territory. Though she had spent only a quick weekend in the mountain town of Asheville, North Carolina, a few days before, the bustling city and the centrally located Battery Park Hotel had started to seem like a home base of sorts.

It was July 1936, and the slim, blond teenager was eager to travel. She had just finished her freshman year at New York University, and the native Staten Islander had never seen the American South.

Helen's father, Joseph, had concocted the plan for Helen's bachelor uncle to escort her across the Old North State that summer. "We were devoted pals, and for fear I was binding my daughter too much to my life and ideas, I arranged for her to visit her relatives in North Carolina and travel some with her Uncle Billy," Joseph explained to a friend.[1] Billy, or William as he was known in professional circles, worked as a dairy extension specialist at North Carolina State College. When classes were out of session, he traveled to inspect and advise dairies across the state on the "newest and best methods for making ice cream, cheese, and butter."[2]

Though William "had not seen much of [Helen] since she was a child," when his brother wrote asking if Helen could accompany him as he completed his summer dairy work, William readily agreed. Joseph told William that Helen "had been working hard in school," and Joseph "wanted her to have the advantage of travel…and the opportunity to meet some of [William's] friends." Helen quickly warmed up to her uncle. "She was becoming sweeter and sweeter to me every day," he said of the young woman.[3]

# 1935

## Valedictorian

**HELEN CLEVENGER**

Valedictorian; A r i s t a member; Editor-in-chief of "Digest"; Latin 3 years award; ice cream counter salesgirl; Class Day Chairman; secretary of Debating Club,; Math. Certificate.

"Attempt the end and never stand to doubt;
Nothing's so hard, but search will find it out."

## The Clock

There's nothing really strange about a clock
Just analyze, you'll realize
It's only wheels and pendulum,
In short, a mechanical thing.
But yet it seems alive; listen to it
Tick-tock, Tick-tock.
There's something harsh and cruel about a clock
It isn't just the clock itself,
So steady, inexorable—
It's time itself, so slow, yet quick,
Ticking our lives away with its measured stroke
Tick-tock, tick-tock.
　　　　　　　　　—HELEN CLEVENGER, '34.

*Left*: Helen Clevenger, senior class, Tottenville High School (Staten Island, New York) yearbook, the *Purple Parrot*, 1935. *Tottenville Historical Society, Staten Island, New York.*

*Above*: "The Clock," a poem written by Helen Clevenger, published in the 1934 edition of the Tottenville High School (Staten Island, New York) yearbook, the *Purple Parrot*. *Tottenville Historical Society, Staten Island, New York.*

Helen's mother, Mary, was not as keen as her husband for their daughter to spend the summer traveling to "strange towns with strange people." "I didn't want her to go," Mary said, "but then you know how mothers are. I was always afraid to let her out of sight. I begged her not to leave me at first, but she was so anxious to go I finally consented." Helen dismissed her mother's concerns: "Oh, mother, I'm no baby. I can take care of myself."[4]

So, Helen traveled south, arriving in the state capital of Raleigh at the beginning of July to first visit with another of her father's brothers, Clinton, who also taught at North Carolina State. She spent her days in Raleigh swimming at the college pool, playing chess with her uncle and waking up early to get in a game of tennis before the temperature rose. After a few days of relaxation, Helen repacked her belongings, and she and William set out.

The first week of the trip was a whirlwind. Beginning July 6, Helen and William traveled from Raleigh in the center of the state to North Carolina's coast, back to Raleigh and then circumnavigated the northwestern part of the state before arriving in Asheville at the Battery Park Hotel on Friday, July 10.[5]

A budding writer and the valedictorian of her high school class, Helen had served as editor-in-chief of the school's newspaper and published poems in the yearbook. As she traveled, she took time every day to carefully record her experiences in her diary and pen lengthy letters to her family and friends. After her first full day in Asheville, Helen wrote her parents, catching them up on what she had done since leaving Raleigh.

> *Dear Mom and Dad,*
>
> *…Uncle Billy and I started on our trip West. Went through Durham and stopped at Burlington where I went through the plant and had a chocolate ice cream cone. At Greensboro I saw butter cut and milk bottled. At High Point I saw ice cream made and ice pops. We had ice cream fresh from the beater and also ice cream pop at Lexington.*
>
> *I had a bottle of orangeade and a dipper of peach ice cream. Thursday night, we stopped at Lenoir at a sort of boarding house.*
>
> *Yesterday, Friday, we had a lovely trip. We traveled through the Blue Ridge Mountains all day. The scenery was beautiful. The highest elevation we were on all day was about 4,247 feet. Stopped at Blowing Rock a point of interest where we climbed up sort of a [ladder] and had a sweeping view of the mountains.*
>
> *We stopped for a while at Sugar Grove where we saw an operating cheese factory run by a Mr. Grant who said, "I feel sorry for anyone who has to return to New York." He told me he had been to New York.*
>
> *We also stopped at West Jefferson where I saw cheese made at a Kraft Phoenix factory. I've got the process written down in my diary but I'm not sure it's exactly right and I'll tell you more about it when I get home.*
>
> *We then drove back on our tracks stopping at Blowing Rock for lunch. Drove through some beautiful mountains and arrived in Asheville about 6:30….*
>
> *Uncle Billy is working this morning and I'll have some time to myself, so I'm catching up with my correspondence. I'll write you again soon….*
>
> *Lots of love to both of you.*[6]

After two full days in the city, a Battery Park bellhop loaded Helen and her uncle's luggage into the trunk of William's car and the pair traveled farther west, visiting the small towns scattered around southwestern North Carolina. They arrived back in Asheville on July 14 and checked back into the fashionable resort hotel.

Less than thirty-six hours later, William discovered Helen's lifeless body crumpled on the floor of her hotel room.[7] But Helen was not the only one to lose her life from the events that unfolded at the Battery Park in the early morning hours of July 16, 1936. Her death became a strand in a tangled knot of politics, police brutality and systemic racism that would, before the end of the year, entrap another young soul.

ASHEVILLE'S NEW BATTERY PARK Hotel sat in the same location (albeit forty feet lower), just northwest of the heart of downtown Asheville, as the original Battery Park Hotel, which had been a sprawling Queen Anne–style, five-hundred-room resort hotel. The first hotel, perched on the top of Battery Porter—a former Confederate battery—boasted

The original Battery Park Hotel, circa 1920. *E.M. Ball Photographic Collection, D.H. Ramsey Library Special Collections, UNC–Asheville, 28804.*

incredible views of the surrounding mountains and was considered to be the height of luxury at the time.[8]

It was built in 1886, and the opening of the "sprawling, turreted" hotel coincided with the arrival of the Western North Carolina Railroad. Along with the railroad came an influx of tourists. And as Asheville's reputation as a tourist destination grew, so did its population. The small town of 2,500 in the 1870s became a bustling city of more than 50,000 residents by 1930.[9]

In 1922, nearly a decade after he built the nearby Grove Park Inn—a competing resort hotel—Edwin Wiley Grove bought the Battery Park. Grove initially intended for the hotel to remain as it was. In a letter to the hotel's previous owner, he wrote, "It is my idea to continue Battery Park Hotel as strictly a resort hotel keeping it open only for the winter and summer seasons."[10]

But not long after, Grove decided that the resort hotel was "rapidly outgrowing its period of usefulness."[11] He razed not only the hotel but also the hill upon which it stood, relocating fifty thousand cubic yards of soil in the process to create additional flat land in Asheville's mountainous

Workers level the hill with steam shovels in front of old Battery Park Hotel, January 1, 1923. *E.M. Ball Photographic Collection, D.H. Ramsey Library Special Collections, UNC–Asheville, 28804.*

downtown area. Battery Park Hill became Battery Park Plaza, and at its apex, sat the new 14-story, 220-room hotel. Even without Battery Park Hill, the new hotel was—and still is—a topographic landmark towering over the downtown area.[12]

Many of Asheville's longtime residents, including Asheville-born novelist Thomas Wolfe, were not impressed. In his semi-autobiographical novel, *You Can't Go Home Again*, Wolfe wrote:

*An army of men and shovels had advanced upon this beautiful green hill and had leveled it down to an ugly flat of clay, and had paved it with a desolate horror of white concrete, and had built stores and garages and office buildings and parking spaces—all raw and new—and were now putting up a new hotel beneath the very spot where the old one had stood. It was to be a structure of sixteen stories* [fourteen actually], *of steel and concrete and pressed brick. It was being stamped out of the same mold, as if by some gigantic biscuit-cutter of hotels that had produced a thousand others like it all over the country.*[13]

But over the next decade, Asheville's residents and visitors began to embrace the new hotel, which hosted F. Scott Fitzgerald (usually under an assumed name), O. Henry and, eventually, even Thomas Wolfe.[14]

It was not hard to see why. Battery Park's brick façade combined neoclassical elegance with a hint of Spanish romanticism. Extending from the east and west elevations of the T-shaped tower were two wings of two stories each. Guests could exit French doors from either of the wings onto terraces surrounded by a balustrade and shaded by a pergola with Ionic columns.[15]

The main body of the hotel rose solidly from the earth for thirteen stories before tapering at the roofline for a fourteenth-story penthouse complete with three large arched windows protected by iron balconies.[16]

The hotel, like most places across the South in the 1930s, abided by Jim Crow laws and racial segregation. People of color could not book a room at the hotel, nor would they be hired to fulfill any of the well-paying positions.

Booker T. Sherrill, one of Battery Park's many Black employees, remembered, "Asheville was hit hard by the Depression. During those times there weren't many jobs open to Blacks—chauffeuring, working at Oteen [Veteran's Hospital] or in hotels....Work was hard to find, but I worked in...the Battery Park from 1934 until it closed in 1972. When I

The new Battery Park Hotel, circa 1924, with George Vanderbilt Hotel in the background and the Grove Arcade at right. *E.M. Ball Photographic Collection, D.H. Ramsey Library Special Collections, UNC–Asheville, 28804.*

worked at the Battery Park, for thirty-eight years, Blacks couldn't go in the front door."[17]

Though only in full operation for a year prior to the crash, the Battery Park—catering primarily to wealthy tourists—weathered the downturn better than most, and by the mid-1930s, when Helen arrived with her uncle Billy, the entire city had more or less recovered financially.[18]

HELEN HAD SPENT THE past year studying in Manhattan and had surely seen the exterior of much larger and more ornate hotels, but Battery Park was the first big hotel where she had ever stayed overnight.

Walking through the front doors for the first time, Helen must have been struck by the lobby, a "splendid, light open-space overlooked on three sides by the paneled balcony of the mezzanine…carried on elaborate ceiling high pillars and ornate consoles."[19]

After crossing the rose and taupe chenille rugs placed to warm the tile-floored lobby, perhaps Helen sat to wait for her uncle to check them in on

Battery Park Hotel interior, circa 1924. *North Carolina Collection, Pack Memorial Public Library, Asheville, North Carolina.*

one of the lobby's "beautiful and harmonious fittings—deep lounges, comfy love seats and dignified pilaster chairs, all made in North Carolina."[20]

"And what a ritzy place we are staying at Battery Park Hotel," Helen wrote to her parents the first morning of her stay. "I have a lovely room and bath on the third floor and you can just bet I took a nap too. We had supper in the dining room of the hotel. Fried scallop, egg plant, carrots, peas, iced tea, and finger bowls. We sat out in front a while. There is a lovely breeze up from the mountains. I wrote my journal last night and then stumbled into bed and slept like a top."[21]

Helen and her uncle left Asheville and the Battery Park on Friday, July 10, to visit dairies farther west. In Murphy, North Carolina, the pair stayed at the Dickey Hotel. The female proprietor described Helen as "reserved, refined and very young looking." Two other young women boarding at the hotel visited with Helen during her stay. "She talked about many things, but she mentioned her diary many times," one of the young women said.[22]

Helen was likely still exhausted when she and William finally arrived back in Asheville around 7:00 p.m. on Tuesday evening, so after having supper in the hotel's dining room, she excused herself and went to her room. Her new room, 224, was virtually identical to the small room on the third floor she had slept in only a few nights before.[23]

Fishing the key from her purse, she unlocked the door and quickly bypassed the doorway to her private bath. Helen placed her purse on the writing desk and tucked several postcards into her diary. After readying for bed, she hung her dress in the wardrobe and finally stretched out on the small but comfortable bed and slept.[24]

After an uneventful night's rest, Helen roused herself to answer the ringing telephone at the foot of her bed, a wake-up call from the front desk. She dressed quickly, pulling on a blue seersucker dress, and met her uncle in the dining room. It would be another full day. After a hearty breakfast, the pair left the city and made the twenty-mile drive to Marshall to attend a farmer's meeting and picnic.[25]

It was a long day, and when the pair arrived back at the hotel, they "went to [their] rooms and cleaned up." William remembered, "I was not in my

Brothers Clinton (*left*) and William Clevenger, 1936. *International News Photo, author's collection.*

13

room much more than an hour anyway. My niece was there about the same time, for we came down and went to supper about 7 o'clock and then drove to the Pegram home as he had invited me out."[26]

Calvin W. Pegram, who knew William from his dairy work, lived in Fairview, about twelve miles from the hotel. Helen enjoyed the visit, later writing in her diary that the Pegrams were "charming people."[27]

But it was getting late, and William planned for them to visit more dairies the following day. Calvin walked with them through the dark to William's car. By the time the pair had driven the narrow country roads back to the hotel, it was nearly 11:00 p.m. William parked out front and locked the car doors. They quickly climbed the hotel's front steps, barely noticing the rain clouds gathering in the darkness. Other guests milled about the lobby, but the pair did not stop to chat.

Side by side they walked to the elevators. William asked the bellboy to take them to the second floor. On the short ride up, Helen exclaimed, "You know so many nice people, Uncle Billy!" amazed at the special treatment she had received at every stop. They agreed to meet at 8:00 a.m. the following morning for breakfast at the hotel. William told Helen he would call the front desk to set a wake-up call for them for 7:30 a.m.[28]

The elevator bell dinged, and the bellboy slid the doors open. "Good night, dear," William said as he walked toward his room just two doors down. Helen bid him goodnight, turned the opposite direction and disappeared around the corner, heading toward room 224.[29]

Even at night, the Battery Park Hotel teemed with life. The early morning hours of Thursday, July 16, 1936, were no exception. As the night watchman made his hourly rounds, guests stumbled through the front doors and bellboys escorted them up to their floors on the elevators.

McGrady Richeson, visiting Asheville from nearby Charlotte, climbed into bed at 11:00 p.m. A summer storm rolled in. Wind, rain and lightning bombarded the hotel. The normal sounds of the city on a summer night were muffled by the storm. When a thunderclap woke Richeson, he made his way into the bathroom to relieve himself and then heard a knock.[30]

"Come in," he called. The knocking persisted. "Come in," he said again, a little more loudly.[31]

The knocking continued. Richeson walked to the door, turned the lock and pulled the door open. Directly across the hall, standing in front of room 224 was a short, stocky young white man wearing a "brown sport

Helen Clevenger, circa 1936. *North Carolina Collection, Pack Memorial Public Library, Asheville, North Carolina.*

coat, brown and white striped sport pants and…a panama hat." When the man saw Richeson, he turned, ran down the hall and disappeared.[32]

ALONE IN HER ROOM, Helen began to wind down for the day. While she had been out, a maid had tidied the room, replaced the candlestick on the mirrored dresser, refilled the water pitcher and provided several clean glasses. Helen took off her shoes and carefully placed them under the upholstered chair by the bed, slipping her feet into a pair of house shoes. She rinsed out her undergarments in the sink, hanging them on the side of the bathtub to dry overnight. Pulling her green silk pajamas from her open bag on the luggage rack, she dressed for bed.[33]

But she did not want to forget the day's events, so she perched at the mahogany desk to make a short entry in her little brown diary. She had already written about her time in Marshall when she had come back to the hotel earlier in the day to change for dinner, so her 10:30 p.m. entry was only six lines. Noting her visit to the Pegram family, she scribbled, "Enjoyed evening very much—lovely people."[34]

With one task accomplished, Helen pulled out a postcard to pen a short note to her mother. She began by asking after her father and her floppy-eared terrier, Duke.

She was scheduled to return to her family's new two-story bungalow in Great Kills, Staten Island, in just a couple weeks. She told her mother that she hoped there would still be ripe huckleberries to pick. She asked about Howard Lally, her friend and a fellow student who was working as a part-time busboy back home. She wanted her mother to know she was having a wonderful time.[35] She closed with the note, "Mother, save these cards. I want to keep them for my souvenirs."[36]

Helen licked a one-cent stamp, affixed it to the postcard and placed it in her white pocketbook to drop in the mail slot in between the elevators in the morning. She left her diary open on the desk.[37]

Having accomplished all she could for the day, Helen kicked off her slippers and placed them under the bed. She removed her wristwatch, laying it gently on the bedside chair. She kept on her ring, inscribed with the phrase "Allaha Abha," a signifier of her Baha'i faith. Relaxing on the bed, she flipped through a magazine by the light of a metal-shaded lamp clamped to the headboard. It was just after 1:00 a.m. Thunder rumbled through the mountains outside her window, muting the sound of footsteps approaching her door.[38]

"OH, MOTHER! OH—" CAME a scream through the wall between rooms 224 and 225 around 1:00 a.m. One of 225's occupants, Nettie M. Cowdin, lay still, straining to hear more. A dull, muffled sound—was that a gunshot? And then nothing.[39]

Her roommate, Lydia Everson, also heard the "sharp, piercing scream" that sounded like "water pitchers and glasses falling." But then she "heard a man's voice, cultured and soft-spoken saying, 'Just a minute and you'll be alright, Molly.'"[40] Relieved, she returned to slumber, content in the knowledge that a husband was soothing his wife after a nightmare.[41]

Nettie stayed awake, not so sure that all was well. She listened for the elevator moving, staying awake for another hour. She heard nothing else.[42]

MRS. GEORGE T. HAYNES in room 223, visiting from Miami, Florida, awoke to screams coming from the room next to hers. The screams stopped. She heard a door close. She lay awake for two more hours, nervous but unwilling to wake her slumbering husband by getting out of bed, turning on the light or calling the front desk.[43]

MISS H.E. JOHNSON, THE assistant housekeeper, lay in bed in room 126, where she had been living since being hired a few weeks earlier. She heard a woman scream somewhere above her. She soon fell asleep.[44]

"PLEASE!" A WOMAN'S VOICE, half pleading, half crying.

"Shut up!" A man's voice, gruff, coarse.

William C. Gatlin sat in the room—No. 324—of his potential employer, A.L. Curtis of Quality Paper Company of Brooklyn, New York, discussing

Room 224 on the northeast exterior of the Battery Park Hotel, July 1936. Though there was some discussion of an intruder walking or crawling into Helen's room on the coping below her window, nothing came of it. *E.M. Ball Photographic Collection, D.H. Ramsey Library Special Collections, UNC–Asheville, 28804.*

a job, when they heard a disturbance. First, a pop—like someone being hit over the head with a glass soda bottle—and then voices, three heavy blows and several "severe, painful moans…getting weaker each time…that lasted about a minute…until it just finished."[45]

Gatlin remarked to Curtis that they should go see what was wrong.

It was probably "someone whipping his wife—or someone else's wife," Curtis replied, but agreed that he would check with the front desk when he went down to mail a few letters and reports.[46]

ERWIN B. PITTMAN, a thirty-two-year-old state bank examiner, stood in his underwear at the sink in his hotel room—number 220—a toothbrush in his mouth, the bathroom door open.

He was visiting Asheville for work and had just finished inspecting the Citizens banks in nearby Marshall and Hot Springs. It had taken him until past 11:00 p.m. to finish comparing notes with his associate, C.W. Calhoun, on the inspections so that he could head home in the morning, but—for now—Pittman was ready to retire for the day.

Before he could fall into bed, a woman's scream broke through the noise of the thunderstorm pounding against the hotel's windows. Three screams came in quick succession. Pittman rushed to the door and threw it open. No one was there. Everything was quiet inside the hotel. Realizing his state of undress, Pittman went back inside, grabbed a bathrobe, knotted it at his waist and returned to the threshold.

He listened. As his eyes adjusted to the hallway's dim light, he made out the figure of a man standing in the doorway across the hallway and slightly to the right of his own.

"I wonder what that noise was?" Pittman said. He paused but got no reply from the shadow in the doorway.

"It sounded like someone was in pain. I wonder where it could be?" Pittman asked, looking toward the figure partly obscured behind the adjacent door.

"That is what I was wondering myself," the "stocky" man replied in a "cultured" voice.[47]

Erwin B. Pittman, 1936. *Associated Press photograph, author's collection.*

Satisfied that the man across the hall was a guest who knew nothing more of the alarming sounds than he did, Pittman shut his door and slept.[48]

THE PHONE AT THE Battery Park's front desk rang. T. Carl Scruggs, the hotel's night clerk, answered.[49] One of their female guests, staying in room 123, had been awakened by a woman's scream. She thought the screams came from the floor above her room. The night watchman was out on his rounds. Scruggs held the message for his return.[50]

IN THE BELLHOPS' SERVICE room off the south side of the lobby, Durham Jones, one of the two bellboys on duty, drank a glass of lemonade just after 1:00 a.m.[51] Suddenly, a man he thought was the hotel's night engineer ran from the stairwell, across the lobby and into the manager's glass-walled office at one corner of the large room.[52] Thinking the engineer was in a rush to close the office's exterior door to keep the rain from coming in, he watched him somewhat casually. But when the man stooped behind the assistant manager's desk, Jones realized the man might be an intruder. "Wonder what that man done?" Jones thought. "He was in an awful hurry."[53] But as he walked toward the office, the screen door leading out to the porch opened, slammed shut, and the man was gone.[54] Night clerk Scruggs saw him too and ran to the front porch, but after losing sight of the fleeing figure, Scruggs decided he was just a "loafer" who had been run out of the basement by the night watchman and did not attempt to follow him.[55]

CHARLES "CASEY" JONES, A taxi driver for Blue Bird taxi company (and no relation to Durham Jones), pulled up at the front door of the Battery Park, jogged up the front steps and picked up the phone on the porch to call his dispatcher, Joe Hall, and file a report about the two drunk men he had just dropped off at the Biltmore Avenue Café. He had been concerned they did not have enough money to pay the full fare.[56]

But just as Joe answered, Casey startled at the sound of a nearby door snapping shut. He turned and saw a man run across the porch toward the balcony railing. "Wait a minute," Casey said to Joe as he slammed down the receiver.[57]

DURHAM JONES BURST OUT of the hotel's front door, "Where'd he go?"

"You mean that crazy man? There he is! He's going to jump!" Casey hollered.[58]

THE MAN VAULTED OVER the hotel's balustrade, barely missing a set of stairs and a railing that led to the hotel's on-site basement barbershop. He turned right and ran to O'Henry Avenue at the west side of the hotel, heading north toward Haywood Street, and disappeared into the night.

Though he never got a clear look at the man, Durham estimated that he was about five foot nine and 160 pounds. He wore dark clothes but no hat.

Casey's estimates were similar—under six feet tall, 170 pounds, dark clothes, no hat. Both men thought the fleeing figure was a white man but were not entirely sure. Casey immediately called Joe Hall back. His first question was, "What time is it?"

Joe answered, "Six minutes past one."[59]

MINUTES LATER, THE HOTEL'S night fireman, C.T. Wilson, strolled into the lobby. Still amped up, Durham and Casey told him about the man vaulting the balustrade and pointed Wilson in the direction he had gone. Wilson hustled down the front steps and around the side of the building. He continued up the alley behind the hotel but saw no one. Relieved that his car was still in its parking place in the alleyway and had not been stolen, Wilson returned to the hotel.[60]

DAVID BOYD, A NEWSPAPER street sales boy, walked north up O'Henry Avenue, heading in the direction of the Battery Park Hotel shortly after 1:00 a.m. A short and heavy man ran toward him through the rain.

"Buy a paper?" Boyd asked.

"I don't have time to read a paper," came the reply.[61]

MEANWHILE, THE HOTEL'S NIGHT watchman, Daniel H. Gaddy, was on his way down to the lobby after completing his 1:00 a.m. hourly inspection of the hotel. As was his routine, Gaddy began his rounds at about five minutes before the hour, starting at the roof level and making his way down to each floor via the stairway. After walking the corridor, Gaddy punched a time clock at the end of each hallway, indicating that he had completed his check of the floor and all was well. He arrived back in the lobby at 1:15 a.m., at least ten minutes after Scruggs received the call about the woman's scream.[62]

When Gaddy checked in with the front desk, Scruggs said, "Somebody called down about a disturbance on the second floor."[63]

"I just came from that floor and everything's all right," Gaddy replied, a little perturbed at being asked to go back up to a floor he had just finished monitoring.[64] Nonetheless, he asked Durham Jones to take him back up to the second floor in the elevator.

Durham and Gaddy pressed their ears to each door on the hallway but heard nothing. Chalking it up to a false alarm—guests often reported hearing noises during the night—the pair returned to the lobby to assure Scruggs that nothing was amiss.[65]

At around 2:00 a.m., a man limped to the door of Gardner Hospital, a small, private institution for white patients in West Asheville—about two and a half miles from the Battery Park Hotel. He spoke briefly to the nurse on duty and asked to be treated for injuries to his legs. She told him he would need to be treated by Dr. Gardner, who was at his home nearby.

When the man arrived at Gardner's house, the doctor sent him back to the hospital with instructions to have the nurse call him when the patient was checked in and ready to be treated.

The man—who had not given his name—never returned to the hospital. Neither the doctor nor the nurse made a note of his physical appearance.[66]

A.L. Curtis, after finishing up a report to send to his office in New York, ventured down to the lobby, envelope in hand. He asked one of the bellboys whether the hotel offered mail delivery to the post office.

"No, sir."

"Is it still raining very hard?"

"No, lightly," came the bellboy's reply.

Curtis walked to the post office, dropped his mail and returned to the hotel about 4:00 a.m. On his way back to his room, he stopped at the front desk to keep his word to his colleague William Gatlin.

"What was the cause of the disturbance a few hours ago?"

"We tried to find out what it was but could not," the night clerk replied.

"I thought it was in a room either on the same floor or below me, but I could get no satisfaction as to what it was," Curtis complained.

Night watchman Gaddy came over to consult with the pair. Curtis described what he heard, but the men could come to no conclusion.[67]

Back in his room, Curtis called Gatlin and told him, "Evidently someone had a nightmare."

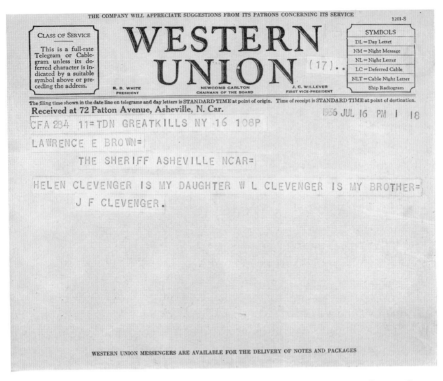

Telegram from Joseph Clevenger to Sheriff Lawrence Brown, July 16, 1936. *Laurence Brown Papers, Swannanoa Valley Museum & History Center, Black Mountain, North Carolina.*

Gatlin replied, "People don't hit themselves with pop bottles when they are having nightmares."[68]

JOSEPH F. CLEVENGER AWOKE in his Staten Island home with an uneasy feeling in his stomach. He had dreamed of his daughter twice the previous night. Both dreams, though no longer "fixed in his mind," were unsettling. He left for work despondent. When his wife, Mary, called him later that day to tell him she had received a telegram from the sheriff of Buncombe County, he did not wait to learn the details but immediately dropped the receiver and headed home.[69]

He answered the telegram, which asked about his relationship to Helen and William Clevenger, at 1:08 p.m. Ten minutes later, his reply came through the Western Union telegraph office in Asheville.[70]

For the next two hours, Joseph and Mary waited for a reply from the sheriff. What had happened? Was Helen hurt? Or perhaps William?[71]

The house telephone rang. It was a member of the Associated Press.[72]

# 2

# OH, IT IS AWFUL! IT IS AWFUL! WHAT IS DONE.

When William Clevenger woke up Thursday morning and looked at his wristwatch, he was relieved to find that it was only 6:00 a.m. He still had another hour and a half before the front desk would call to rouse him from bed.[73]

Still, 7:30 a.m. came and went and the telephone in his room never rang. Slightly annoyed to have to wake himself after all the aggravation he had gone through the evening prior to set up the morning call, William went about his routine. He bathed, dressed, put on his hat and was out the door by 8:20 a.m. Realizing that his niece likely did not receive a wake-up call either, he decided to knock on her door on his way down to breakfast.[74]

Bypassing the bank of elevators, William rounded the corner and passed the stairwell and the closed door to room 225 on his left. He briefly acknowledged the hotel's carpenter, Henry H. Laetsche, and a maid, Evelyn Moss, who were in the midst of their daily rounds.[75] William lightly rapped on door 224, expecting Helen to reply "Hello?" as she normally did when he arrived to escort her to breakfast or supper, but no reply came. He knocked harder. Still there was no response.[76]

"Helen," he called. When there was again no answer from his niece, William's "heart went to [his] mouth." He "grabbed hold of the doorknob, shook it," hoping to wake her. The knob turned; the door was not locked as it should have been. It swung open to a point, stopping abruptly; there was something in the way.[77]

Stepping into the room, peering around the half-open door, William saw his worst fear—Helen, still clad in her green silk pajamas, lay in the room's small hallway, her legs folded beneath her supine and bloodied body. Falling to his knees beside his niece, William grabbed Helen and shook her. Realizing then that the situation was dire, William rushed into the hallway yelling, "Oh, it is awful! It is awful! What is done."[78]

Henry and Evelyn looked up from their work at the panic-stricken man. "Go look in there and see what they have done to her," William told them in desperation.[79] The carpenter immediately went to the room and saw Helen "lying on her back, with [her] legs doubled under her thighs."[80] Evelyn stayed in the hall. She had, not ten minutes before, checked Helen's door and recorded that it was locked from the inside on her housekeeping form.[81]

Henry quickly closed the door and crossed the hall, letting himself into a vacant room to call the hotel manager's office.[82] The assistant manager, Raymond R. "Ray" McComas, was on duty that morning. Ray rushed to the second floor—the same floor on which he and his wife resided—and entered Helen's room.

"[I] found her body lying near the bathroom door. Her left hand was on her chest, [her] right hand was circled over her head," McComas remembered.[83] An empty .32-caliber shell lay next to her just over the threshold of the white-tiled bathroom. He told William to go back to his room and wait. Then Ray instructed Henry to stand guard at the door while he hurried downstairs to alert the hotel's manager, Patrick "Pat" Henry Branch, who was eating breakfast in the dining room.[84]

SIXTY-THREE-YEAR-OLD PAT BRANCH HAD been in the hotel business since 1889, when he got his start at the old Battery Park Hotel as a teenager, eventually working his way up to the position of clerk at the nearby Kenilworth Inn and then co-manager at Asheville's Berkeley Hotel. By the time he was appointed manager of the new Battery Park Hotel in 1928, Branch had managed or owned some of the most prominent hotels in the Asheville area.[85]

Though the stocky, bespectacled man was nearing the end of a half-a-century-long hotelier career, Branch had never dealt with a suspicious death in one of his hotels. Perhaps that was why he did not immediately call the police. Instead, upon seeing Helen's body, Branch quickly turned and went to the room of the house physician, Dr. David M. Buck Jr.[86]

Patrick H. Branch Sr., circa 1940s. *North Carolina Collection, Pack Memorial Public Library, Asheville, North Carolina.*

"Dr. Buck, it looks like we have found a dead woman down on the second floor in room 224," Branch told the doctor when he answered the door.[87]

By the time Dr. Buck dressed and arrived a good twenty minutes later, it was nearly a quarter to nine.[88] All the while, the hotel's employees waited, no one entirely sure if Helen was still alive.[89]

The assistant manager escorted Dr. Buck into Helen's room. Again, the door "hit an obstacle" when the men tried to push it open. "It [is] pinned against her knee," Dr. Buck explained. Sliding through the partly open door, he took out his stethoscope to listen for a heartbeat. He flashed a light in her eyes, looking for any reaction. He lifted her arm. It was "stiff and rigid." Helen's abdomen was cold. Blood streaked her face, neck and the left side of her chest.[90]

Dr. Buck pronounced Helen Irene Clevenger dead nineteen minutes after her body was found. "She ha[s] been dead about six or seven hours," Dr. Buck concluded.[91]

"I'll call the coroner for you," Dr. Buck told Pat Branch. The group followed the doctor down to the lobby to make the call to the coroner, leaving Henry Laetsche standing sentry at the entrance to room 224. But the coroner was out of the office for the morning, so they waited. And waited.[92]

Finally, thirty-five minutes later, Branch called the sheriff's department. "Send a deputy over to the Battery Park Hotel right away!" the manager exclaimed when Deputy Tom K. Brown answered.

"What's the trouble?" Brown replied.

"We think there's a woman dead over here," Branch told him.[93]

Deputies Tom Brown and Leet Sluder rushed to the hotel, only a short distance from the county courthouse, where the sheriff's office occupied the first floor. Pat Branch met them in the lobby and escorted them to the second floor. Sluder broke off to visit William Clevenger's room and monitor the deeply in-shock professor, while Branch showed Tom Brown to Helen's room.

Branch pulled out his master key to unlock the door to room 224, but as he did so, he realized there was a key already sticking out of the lock. Puzzled, Branch grabbed the key, "Is this yours?" Branch asked Deputy Brown.

"Yes," Tom Brown replied, though he had never seen the key before. He pocketed it as evidence before stepping into the room—the first law enforcement officer on the scene.[94]

Despite the hotel being situated within Asheville city limits and police jurisdiction, the Asheville Police Department did not hear of Helen's death until after 1:00 p.m., when the desk sergeant answered a call from a reporter about a potential crime at the Battery Park. Chief of Police William J. Everett dismissed it as a "wild rumor" and left with Detective Captain Fred Jones to go fishing near Mount Mitchell, about an hour's drive from the city.[95]

It was not until 3:00 p.m. that the desk sergeant called the sheriff's office to check the veracity of the "wild rumor." When he learned that there had, in fact, been a suspicious death, he immediately volunteered police services, but, with the police chief out of town, the sheriff's office had already taken control of the case.[96]

Sheriff's deputies Frank Messer and George W. Garrison joined Deputy Tom Brown at 9:50 a.m. And a little over half an hour later, Tom Brown's brother, Buncombe County sheriff Laurence E. Brown, pulled his armored car up to the hotel's front door.[97]

By 1936, Sheriff Brown was already an institution in Buncombe County. Born in 1895 in the nearby town of Black Mountain, about fifteen miles east

H.M. Morrell, of the Norland-Brown Funeral Home, holds Helen's bloodstained pajama top. At the left, near the top, is the hole made by the bullet. *E.M. Ball Photographic Collection, D. H. Ramsey Library Special Collections, UNC–Asheville, 28804.*

of Asheville, Brown was the son of the minister at the local Baptist church, who also happened to have been the first mayor of the small town.[98]

Both Laurence and his younger brother, Carey, played football at Black Mountain High School and went on to play at the Presbyterian College of South Carolina. But when Carey was paralyzed during a scrimmage in the final months of 1923 and died five days later,[99] Laurence hung up his leather helmet, gave up his dream of becoming a lawyer, moved back home and turned his sights toward law enforcement.[100]

The World War I veteran joined the Buncombe County Sheriff's Department in 1924 as a deputy under Sheriff E.M. Mitchell, who he would—two years later—defeat in the Democratic primary election for sheriff.[101]

On December 6, 1926, Brown, a newlywed thirty-one-year-old who "looked more like a movie hero than a sheriff,"[102] began serving his first term during the height of Prohibition.

From the beginning, Brown waged a war against bootleggers, rumrunners and moonshiners across the county, busting up stills and destroying the livelihoods of many a mountain brewer. By the end of his first full week in office, Brown and his deputies had confiscated 250 gallons of liquor.[103]

That same week, an Asheville men's clothing store ran a Christmas ad in the *Asheville Citizen* that read, "Three more days to do your shopping. We have all the nice things for him except the flask and contents—Sheriff Brown has that—."[104]

By July 1927, the regular storage room at the county courthouse was filled with "countless bottles, fruit jars, jugs, cans, kegs, and barrels stacked in congested confusion…[which had] long since made the sheriff's private office a place of rank atmosphere with the odor of sour sugar liquor."[105]

Laurence E. Brown.
*Laurence Brown Collection, Swannanoa Valley Museum & History Center, Black Mountain, North Carolina.*

In the spring of 1928, Brown announced that he would seek reelection on the Democratic ticket. Soon after his announcement, C.C. Hamby, who had been arrested several times for violating Prohibition laws by the sheriff's department, began posting placards throughout the county alleging Brown accepted bribes as a deputy. Brown denied the allegations, insisting Hamby was perjuring himself at the behest of Brown's opponent in the primary.[106] Still, though Brown easily won the primary, for the first time in thirty-two years, Democrats lost almost every elected position in Buncombe County, including sheriff.[107]

Brown went home to Black Mountain and for the next two years chased down liquor-laden automobiles in the small town as chief of police until he could run for sheriff again in 1930. This time he would not be defeated.[108]

Over the next half decade, Brown began modernizing the sheriff's department. Prior to 1935, the department closed at the end of the regular work day. At Brown's urging, the legislature passed a law requiring deputies to be on duty around the clock. Brown began a uniformed night patrol, purchased submachine guns and an armored car and had a radio system installed in patrol cars that could receive messages from three dispatch points—the sheriff's office, the Asheville Police Department and the county courthouse. The Buncombe County Jail was relocated to the top five floors of the courthouse.[109]

"He was a big man. He stood about 6'4", I guess, and probably hit about 200 pounds or better. He wasn't fat, now, don't get me wrong. He was big!…

never carried a pistol or ever wore a badge," Deputy Jake Robertson said of the sheriff.[110] *Asheville Citizen* reporter Harold Hammond described him a bit differently. "He's tall and straight as a mountain pine, rugged as a laurel thicket, with a face as stern and unyielding as chiseled granite, broken by bushy brows. His eyes burn….No matter how tall you are, you get the feeling he is looking down on you. It's inconceivable that Laurence Brown could have been anything but a sheriff."[111]

The Sheriff Brown who parked in front of the Battery Park Hotel on the morning of July 16, 1936, was forty-one years old and a father of three boys. He had more than a decade of law enforcement experience under his belt, including almost eight years as high sheriff of the county. Still, in less than four months, he would again need to win enough votes to keep his job. Solving a high-profile case quickly could be just the thing to guarantee another two-year term. But failing to solve it prior to the election could have the exact opposite effect.

His approach to law enforcement at the time and the media's reaction to it was perhaps best characterized by an article in the *Charlotte News* celebrating Brown's automobile of choice:

> *A 1934 model Graham supercharger…made at the Indianapolis plant especially for the sheriff's war against bootleggers. Bullet proof glass, almost an inch and three-quarters thick, protects the occupants, and through this glass are sheathed portholes, which can be opened only by the hard thrust of a gun from inside….Radiator, hood and cowl are bullet-proof, lined with special steel, but the front bumper is the most impressive part of the big sedan. It consists of armored plate to protect the front tires from bullets, and a heavy bumper for knocking cars off the road. If he can't make a fleeting car stop any other way, Mr. Brown runs up behind it and smacks it with that mighty prow. Inside are gun racks and pistol holders. The car is equipped with tommy-guns and automatics. No one has ever escaped pursuit.*[112]

When Sheriff Brown—not to be confused with Deputy Sheriff Brown, Laurence's brother, Tom, who was first on the scene (and had been appointed by Laurence as a deputy)—arrived at Helen's Battery Park Hotel room, Deputy Frank Messer stood in the hallway, camera up, capturing an image of Helen sprawled on the floor through the open doorway.

In the black-and-white photograph, "her head was away from the door, knees toward the door with feet bent back under her body. Her hands were

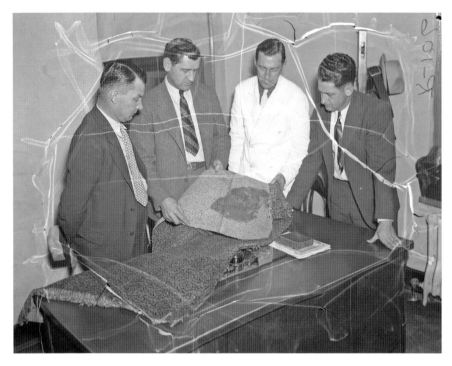

In his office at the county courthouse, Sheriff Laurence Brown (*second from left*) examines a section of carpet stained with Helen's blood, 1936. Others (*from left to right*) are City Detective Robert Patton, Deputy Frank Messer and Deputy Tom Brown. *E.M. Ball Photographic Collection, D.H. Ramsey Library Special Collections, UNC–Asheville, 28804.*

lying something like beside her. Her face was turned a little to the right." Brown waited for Messer to take a few more shots before entering.[113]

Now standing just inside the doorway, Sheriff Brown took stock of the room's condition in the detached, methodical way of a professional. "The bed…was turned down from the head, and looked as if it had been sat on. There was a chair by the side of the bed. There were red stains, like bloody fingerprints, on that chair. There was a slip on the back of the chair. Her watch was on that chair, her wrist watch.[114]

"There was a baggage rack by the side of the body, with a suitcase open on it. There was a diary on the writing table. It was open. There was a postcard there. The bathroom door was open, and in the bathroom there was a brassiere on the bathtub. Straightened out on the bathtub. It had [been recently washed]."[115]

Stooping to kneel over Helen's body, Brown noted a gunshot wound in her chest. "Around the wound it looked as if there was some powder burns and outside for an inch and a half there were burns, slight burns, all the way around for an inch and a half. On the inside of the wound there were powder burns, inside the wound pretty deep."[116]

On the other side of the room, Deputy George Garrison had already begun dusting for fingerprints. He started with a light bulb that had been found lying in the chair beside the bed. The bulb had been removed from its fixture, but the light switch was still engaged; Garrison guessed that someone who was unfamiliar with the switch had unscrewed the light bulb to darken the room.

"Nope, not a single clear print," Garrison reported to the sheriff. "All smudges and smear. I would have given odds of 100 to 1 I'd find something clear as crystal on the light bulb. But—and I don't know whether he was smart or lucky—he unscrewed the bulb with the circle formed by his thumb and forefinger, not the thumb and finger alone. Didn't touch his finger-tips to the globe at all."

"How about the key found in the door?" one of the deputies asked.

Helen Clevenger's room (224) at the Battery Park Hotel, 1936. The folded blanket on the floor in the hallway indicates where Helen's body was found *E.M. Ball Photographic Collection, D H. Ramsey Library Special Collections, UNC–Asheville, 28804.*

Helen Clevenger's death certificate, 1936. *North Carolina State Board of Health, Bureau of Vital Statistics.*

"No luck there either," Garrison replied.[117]

There was no sign of a struggle and no sign of a weapon. Still, it did not take long for the sheriff's department to label Helen's death a murder. And when the county coroner finally did arrive and later conduct an autopsy, he came to the same conclusion.[118]

From the angle at which the bullet passed through her body, penetrating her upper left lung, investigators conjectured that she had been on her knees, potentially begging the gunman for her life, when shot with what was believed to be a .32-caliber automatic pistol. The gun had been pressed to her breast so closely that the gunpowder burned her skin.

Helen had lived for almost fifteen minutes after being shot, long enough that her killer had struck her several times across the face with a sharp instrument—potentially in an attempt to stop her from screaming. Stab wounds penetrated her face below her left eye, to the side of her nose and through the roof of her mouth. She eventually died from blood loss in the early morning hours of July 16, 1936.[119]

HELEN'S MURDER MADE THE front page above the fold in Asheville's evening newspaper, the *Asheville Times*, less than twelve hours after her body was discovered. Before long, reporters had flown in from Raleigh, Atlanta, New York and Baltimore to cover the investigation and wire stories back to their home papers.[120]

Much of what is known about the day-to-day investigation into Helen's murder comes from the yellowing pages of Asheville's daily newspapers, which reported—sometimes in minute detail—every kernel of information they could glean by staking out the county courthouse, the hotel and the funeral home.

No detail was too small to be reported—including an altercation between a local reporter, Doug Eller, and police captain Fred Jones. After the *Asheville Citizen* published an article about the police chief's fishing trip, Captain Jones found Eller outside the courthouse. He shouted, advancing on the man, an open knife in hand, "Why you dirty double-crossing ———. If you get on your feet I will whip you ——— you, until you can't stand up. The whole damn outfit has a yellow streak a mile wide down its back and you can go back over there and tell your bosses I said so. I am not afraid of a damn one of your gang."[121]

That day, the chief of police assigned five city police detectives to aid the sheriff with the investigation into Helen's death—Captain Jones among them.[122]

THE PRESS ALSO DESCENDED on the Clevengers' Staten Island home.[123] Helen's father was already on his way to Asheville, but her mother, who was "an invalid…unable to leave her…home,"[124] took reporters' questions as she "sobbed on the shoulder of a neighbor woman who came to comfort her." Clutching the telegram from Sheriff Brown informing her of Helen's murder, which she received only after learning of her daughter's death from reporters, the gray-haired woman spoke through her tears, "Maybe it's not so."

A beat later, she asked her friend, "No, the police wouldn't say it was so if it wasn't, would they?"

"Helen was a bright girl," Mary told the reporters, "Do you know she was valedictorian a year ago when she graduated from Tottenville High School? And she won two scholarships to the university."

Steeped in grief, Mary paced the floor in the dimly lit room with the blinds drawn.

Joseph and Mary Clevenger look at an album containing photographs of their daughter, Staten Island, New York, July 28, 1936. *North Carolina Collection, Pack Memorial Library.*

"This might have happened anyway," she said. "If she had gone to camp she might have been drowned or been in an accident."

Finally, Mary's neighbor escorted the reporters from the house, urging her friend to rest.[125]

WHILE SHERIFF BROWN AND his deputies gathered evidence, the Asheville Police Department, perhaps to cover their embarrassment at not being the lead investigators on the case, made an arrest. Police officers arrived at the Battery Park at 11:03 p.m., less than forty-eight hours after the murder, and escorted Joe B. Ury, a thirty-one-year-old bellhop, to the city jail, denying him bond. Suspicion fell on Ury, "a tall, light-colored negro, [who wore] glasses and ha[d] a small moustache" and was considered to be "somewhat of an athlete"[126] because the year before, "Ury, allegedly, had led a salesman

Joe Ury, circa 1936. *E.M. Ball Photographic Collection, D.H. Ramsey Library Special Collections, UNC–Asheville, 28804.*

to the room of a young woman, who later brought sensational charges against her visitor."[127] Police chief Everett thought that perhaps Helen's murderer could have found his way to the room in a similar fashion, so Ury spent the evening in jail on an "investigation charge."[128]

Early the next morning, officers searched Ury's home for any evidence that could potentially link him with the crime. They left carrying a men's shirt with a suspicious stain on the shoulder.

Chief Everett "subject[ed] the Negro to an extensive grilling."[129] Ury vehemently denied having any knowledge of the murder. He maintained that he left the hotel in a taxi about half an hour after his shift ended at midnight the night Helen was killed.

Officers sent Ury back to a cell while they checked his alibi and waited for the test results on the stained shirt.

It did not take long to track down Ury's taxi driver. After a brief interview, in which the cabbie told police that he picked up Ury at Battery Park and dropped him off at his house a little before 1:00 a.m., the police determined that Ury had been telling the truth.

Though Everett told reporters that he would release Ury that evening, the bellhop spent another night in jail. He was finally released at 2:30 p.m. the following afternoon.[130] With Ury out of police custody, officers also abandoned their plan to analyze the stains on his shirt, instead noting that the stains were likely rust.[131]

A reporter for the *Atlanta Daily World*, a prominent Black-run newspaper, covered the story of Ury's release, writing, "They grilled the arrested young man unrelentlessly, before they finally concluded his alibi was 'air-tight.'… They have since decided that a white slayer was more than probable.… The short space of time between the discovery of the gruesomely shot and stabbed body of the girl and the arrest of the youth," the journalist continued, "show the proneness of certain groups to jump to the conclusion that if a Negro is about when a crime has been committed. 'HE DID IT.'"[132]

"In smaller, more southerly towns," the reporter concluded, "the unfortunately arrested youth would most likely have been lynched before

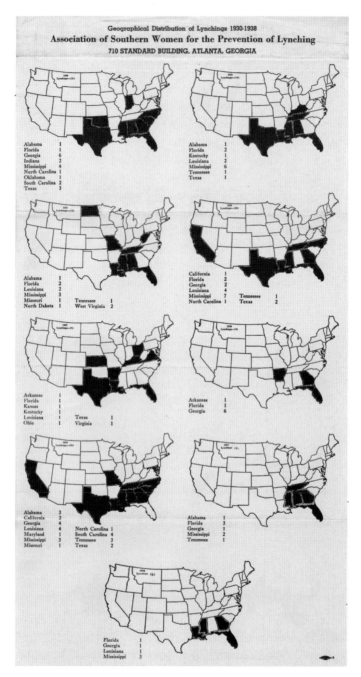

Map showing the distribution of lynchings from 1930 to 1938 in the United States. *Geographical Distribution of Lynchings 1930–1938. Atlanta, Georgia: Association of Southern Women for the Prevention of Lynching, [1939.] archive.org*

intelligent analysis and diagnosis of the crime and its possibilities were made. All the pleadings of 'I didn't do it....I didn't do it!' would have been to no avail. But in this instance, thanks be to God, they listened and Chief of Police William J. Everett is to be commended and congratulated for the orderly manner in which the investigation was carried out, and the prevention of another blot on the American public. Many more have not done 'it'!!"[133]

# 3

# A DATE TONIGHT WITH
# A GIRL AT THE BATTERY PARK

Newspapers and magazines across the nation continued to report that Helen had been "criminally assaulted," even after the coroner's conclusion that Helen had not been raped or sexually assaulted was made public.[134] As a young woman traveling accompanied only by her unmarried uncle, the media and the general public scrutinized any tidbits they could uncover about Helen's personal life and who she may have potentially met up with while in Asheville.

This speculation was fueled by the assertion by the sheriff's department that Helen's murder must have been a "crime of passion."[135] And when Helen's grieving father, Joseph, arrived in Asheville on Friday afternoon, Sheriff Brown summoned him to his office for questioning. Did he know of anyone in Helen's life who had a motive to kill the teenager? Did she have a boyfriend? Had she met any men while visiting North Carolina?[136]

Joseph could think of no one who would wish his daughter harm. He emphasized that it would not have been in Helen's nature to have arranged to meet a man unchaperoned.

But later that day, Sheriff Brown learned that five days before her death, during her first visit to the city, the eighteen-year-old had "spent at least six daylight hours in Asheville unaccompanied by her uncle" while he prepared dairying reports with his colleague Calvin Pegram.[137]

On Saturday morning, July 11, Pegram pulled up to the Battery Park Hotel, where Helen and her uncle were waiting for him out on the expansive hotel porch. Pegram climbed the steps and greeted Helen briefly before

The Battery Park Hotel, circa 1930s. *E.M. Ball Photographic Collection, D.H. Ramsey Library Special Collections, UNC–Asheville, 28804.*

heading back down to the car with William at his side. The two men left Helen sitting alone.

"Just as we were ready to start, Mr. Clevenger and I both turned our eyes towards the girl and noticed she was talking with a taxi cab driver," Pegram later told reporters. "After the murder, I recalled the incident to Mr. Clevenger and we both told it to officers. Apparently she was asking the cab driver for information of some sort."

One reporter from the local paper interviewed a number of local cab drivers as well as the Battery Park's taxi service, but none recalled—or would admit to—speaking with Helen.[138] Police captain Fred Jones and Detective Robert Patton even traveled to one of the western North Carolina cities that Helen and her uncle had visited, acting on a tip that Helen had "mentioned the name of an Asheville man she was supposed to have met." They questioned dozens of people Helen and William had visited, but none recalled her making a statement about a man from Asheville.[139]

After his morning meeting with Pegram, William returned to have lunch with his niece and then left her alone again until dinner. The pair chatted over their meal, but William could not recall exactly what they talked about. He was certain, however, that Helen did not mention meeting any men while unsupervised.[140] Whether she would have confided in her uncle remained a matter of discussion among the general public. Pegram told the press that he did not remember Helen ever "mention[ing] boys...but she made friends easily and was a typical college freshman in her enthusiasm over her courses."[141]

Still, wild speculation about who Helen might have met that day while on her own and, perhaps, arranged to meet on her return to the city continued. As gossip circulated and investigators began taking witness accounts, lugging a heavy typewriter from house to house to collect statements,[142] they received a tip that led to the arrest of a minor local celebrity—a man who had left his wife and child in Washington, D.C., and was known to be a playboy: Mark Wollner.

MARK WOLLNER, A THIRTY-FIVE-YEAR-OLD well-known white German concert violinist, leased a studio in the Grove Arcade across the street from the Battery Park Hotel. He had resided in Asheville for only the past two years but had been in the United States for more than eight, "continuing in New York and Washington a brilliant musical career that started in his native country."[143] He was "a stocky young [man], handsome, blonde, muscular... [who] did not look like a violinist, but more like an athlete."[144]

And on the night of the murder, he was overheard in a downtown cigar shop saying, "I've got a date tonight with a girl at the Battery Park I met two days ago. Guess I'll have to get a lot of wine."[145] The sheriff immediately pursued the lead.

As it happened, Wollner was scheduled to give a concert along with several of his students at Asheville's Grove Park Inn the following evening.[146]

Mark Wollner plays his violin, 1936. *E.M. Ball Photographic Collection, D.H. Ramsey Library Special Collections, UNC–Asheville, 28804.*

Sheriff Brown purchased a ticket for Erwin Pittman, the hotel guest who had spoken to a shadowy figure standing in the threshold of Helen's room the night she was murdered. He had come back into town at the sheriff's request to assist investigators. Pittman soon took his seat in the grand lobby of the great cut-granite hotel, studying Wollner as the violinist introduced his pupils.[147]

"He seems to be about the same build as the man I was talking to [in the doorway to Helen's room], but his voice seems to be a little higher pitched," Pittman told the deputy accompanying him.[148] Still, even without a positive identification, the following morning, officers drove to the Grove Arcade and found Wollner wearing a "checkered sport coat and checkered trousers"[149] in his friend's music shop. The pair were engaged in an intense conversation; the music critic who had reviewed Wollner's recent concert had misspelled the names of several of his musical numbers.[150]

The "dapper, well-dressed" violinist was hustled into the back of a waiting vehicle, ushered quickly to the courthouse and immediately taken to

The Grove Arcade, circa 1930s. The Battery Park Hotel can be seen in the background. *E.M. Ball Photographic Collection, D.H. Ramsey Library Special Collections, UNC–Asheville, 28804.*

speak with officers about how he had spent last Wednesday night and early Thursday morning.[151]

At the news of his detention, the media immediately reached out to Wollner's estranged wife, twenty-nine-year-old language teacher Mary Bowen Wollner. The couple had separated two years prior and had a four-year-old daughter who lived with her mother in Washington, D.C.[152]

Mary lamented, "This is terrible news. Even though I can't believe he is involved, any mention of a musician's name in such a case is damaging."[153]

After being questioned by officers behind closed doors, Wollner signed his statement, and Sheriff Brown allowed several eager reporters in to see the musician so that he could observe Wollner's reaction to questions from the media.[154] As flashbulbs exploded, the press peppered the man with questions.

"I have no statement to make," Wollner replied. "Except to say I have nothing to do with this business."[155]

Wearing a coat with broad checks and a red necktie, Mark Wollner smokes a cigarette at the sheriff's office while detained for questioning, July 20, 1936. *Associated Press photo, author's collection.*

"What business?" Deputy Tom Brown asked sharply. "We haven't accused you of anything."

"I am here because I am a musician. I live only for my music," Wollner replied cryptically to the deputy.

"Then you don't know anything about this murder?" one of the reporters cut in.

"I haven't been near that hotel in six months," Wollner replied.

Deputy Brown, on high-alert for anything suspicious from the violinist, interjected, "What hotel? Nobody mentioned a hotel."

"I do not know why I am here," Wollner answered. "Are you through with me now?"[156]

"Were you at home the night the girl was killed?" a reporter called.

"Oh, is that it?" Wollner replied, refusing further questions.[157]

"I expect you will have to stay with us tonight," Deputy Brown said with some finality.

Wollner stopped to pose for a few photographs before being led to his jail cell for the night.

When officers arrived to question him further, he told them, "I don't know a thing about who murdered that girl. I had nothing at all to do with it. Why, I've never laid eyes on her."[158]

"Did you have a date on Wednesday night, the night of the murder?" the officers asked.

"No, I did not!"

"Yet we have a witness who asserts you told him that you had a date Wednesday night with a girl at the Battery Park. Did you make such a remark?"

"I can't remember ever having said that," Wollner replied.

Still, Wollner had an alibi.

"Then what did you do Wednesday night?" asked Sheriff Brown.

"I went home early, about 9:30, I believe. I talked to Mildred Ward until about 11, when I went to bed. I stayed in bed until 8:00 the next morning."[159]

Wollner boarded at a house at 14 Starnes Avenue in Asheville with Essie Ward and her daughter, Mildred.[160]

Mildred, "a frail, delicate-looking brunette of nineteen,"[161] told detectives that Wollner had been home all night. The young woman, who was residing at home while recuperating from tuberculosis, had previously worked as a waitress before being diagnosed. She told investigators that over the last year she had gone on dates with Wollner "quite often."[162]

She recalled that on Wednesday evening, Wollner returned to the house about 10:00 p.m. and then walked down the street to a café to get her a soda. He returned a few minutes later, they spoke for a while and then around 11:40 p.m. he went to his room on the second floor of the house. Mildred went to her room on the first floor, which she shared with her mother. Though she slept, she and her mother were both light sleepers, and she was positive that she would have heard Wollner if he had left the house during the night.[163]

The following morning, Mildred said, Wollner stopped in the kitchen around 8:00 a.m. on his way out the door, and Essie served him two cups of coffee.[164]

However, other witnesses soon came forward, placing Wollner out and around town on Wednesday night and early Thursday morning. Sheriff Brown felt that these sightings were credible, particularly because Wollner was "a conspicuous figure because of the rather noticeable sport clothes he affected."[165]

The owner of a downtown café saw Wollner eating dinner sometime between 9:00 p.m. and 10:00 p.m. on Wednesday night. A reporter then saw him at a saloon around 10:30 p.m. And at about 2:00 a.m. on Thursday

Mildred Ward at home, circa 1936. *E.M. Ball Photographic Collection, D.H. Ramsey Library Special Collections, UNC–Asheville, 28804.*

morning, an unnamed female saw Wollner walking the downtown streets. He was not seen again until daylight.

Charles English, an employee of a café in downtown Asheville, told the sheriff that he saw Wollner at about 6:15 a.m. on Thursday morning, when the violinist came in for a cup of coffee. Wollner told English, "I have been out all night and had a bad night."[166]

At about 6:30 a.m., "Wollner knocked on the window of Miss Ward's room on the first floor of the residence and then went up the back steps of the house,"[167] Lavada Whitaker, a thirty-year-old neighbor of Essie Ward, told the sheriff. "He walked as though his leg hurt."[168]

"Five hours later I saw Wollner and Miss Ward come on the back porch," Whitaker continued. "Miss Ward tried to keep the man from leaving, but he broke away. He was carrying a pair of trousers under his arm."[169] Mrs. Roy Bailey, who lived at the same residence as Whitaker, corroborated her housemate's story.

Home of Essie and Mildred Ward, 14 Starnes Avenue, Asheville, 1936, with an Asheville police vehicle parked in front. *E.M. Ball Photographic Collection, D.H. Ramsey Library Special Collections, UNC–Asheville, 28804.*

Sheriff Brown began to suspect that Wollner's main alibi witness, Mildred Ward, might be trying to protect the musician, so he brought her in for questioning. Mildred maintained her assertion that she was positive that Mark was home all night the evening of the murder, though she did concede that shortly before officers took him in to custody, he had called her and asked, "Where was I Wednesday evening?"[170]

Hoping that a night in jail might give Mildred time to think, Sheriff Brown placed a cot in the jail matron's quarters. As a concession to her illness, the sheriff called her doctors to the jail to ensure that the matron's quarters would not exacerbate her tuberculosis. When asked about her incarceration, Mildred told reporters that she had no complaints about the jail except to say that the mattress on her bed was too hard.[171]

MEANWHILE, IN THE MEN'S section of the jail, Dr. Howard L. Sumner, the county physician, pulled Wollner from his cell to examine him for bruising at the sheriff's request.[172] He reported back quickly. Wollner's left foot bore a number of suspicious injuries. His left heel was bruised, the underside of one of the toes on his left foot was split open and his instep was scratched.[173]

When this information was released in the papers, the gossip mill ignited. Wollner's injuries could certainly have resulted from vaulting a balustrade and landing hard on the concrete sidewalk below. Though Wollner did not try to defend or explain the injuries to reporters, his friend W.H. Rymer later told them that Wollner was a "very active" musician and that he often had a sore foot from moving back and forth on his feet to keep time with the music as he played violin.[174]

Among the general public and the media, there was considerable discussion about the implications of Wollner rushing home for a new pair of pants just a few hours after the murder. But soon another of Wollner's girlfriends spoke up. Mary Brooks, "his blonde and competent accompanist," recalled that the "incident of the trousers" occurred not on Thursday morning but Friday morning.[175]

Mark Wollner plays violin accompanied by Mary Brooks on piano, 1936. *North Carolina Collection, Pack Memorial Public Library, Asheville, North Carolina.*

"I knew Mr. Wollner for more than 10 months," Brooks told reporters. "He is a fine man, a talented musician, and I never knew anything wrong about him. The incident of the trousers took place, not on the day following the murder, but on the day after."[176]

"Well, he was in a hurry," Brooks conceded. "He was in a hurry because that was Friday afternoon, not long before his concert at the Grove Park Inn. He had to take his dress clothes to a tailor for alteration. I drove him to his house in my car. He ran in and fetched his trousers. I'm definite about that. This incident took place Friday, not Thursday."

She also confided that she had walked around Asheville with him on both Thursday and Friday.[177] "They say he has a bad wound on his foot or leg, which might have been caused by leaping over the 12-foot parapet at the Battery Park Hotel. They are trying to connect him with a man who did make that leap. Well, I had to beg him all morning to walk slower. I couldn't keep up with him. No, he didn't walk at all like a man who had a bad leg."[178]

Still another girlfriend spoke up in Wollner's defense. The unnamed woman related that she was with Wollner when he read of Helen's death in the newspaper and that he showed "not the slightest concern other than ordinary human interest." The following day, she was with him at a drugstore in Asheville and he never mentioned the murder. Instead, he began arguing with another patron at the store, bragging about who could speak more languages.[179]

Those who knew of the local celebrity mostly agreed that the man Pittman spoke to could not have been Wollner unless he had been trying to disguise his voice, since the violinist spoke with a heavy German accent. Had he been dressed as he normally was for a date—dapper in colorful and conspicuous clothing, his "mop of blonde hair" rarely covered with a hat, then surely he would have been easily recognizable to the hotel's guests and employees.[180]

Still, one columnist for the *Asheville Citizen* wrote, "Surmise on [Wollner's] guilt or innocence has been wide-spread with perhaps the majority opinion leaning toward the possibility that in the long run he would be unable to extricate himself from the web of evidence being woven about him by the sheriff's masterly handling of the case."[181]

So, the sheriff held Wollner in jail. Wollner's friend Rymer, the sixty-five-year-old proprietor of the piano shop where Wollner was arrested, showed up that night at the jail to see the violinist and announced he was prepared to put up $20,000 in bond for Wollner's release. He was unsuccessful in both attempts, and Wollner remained alone in his cell.[182]

Exiting the jail, Rymer spoke about his friend, worrying that being held had already done irreparable harm to his reputation in the city. "I am Wollner's friend and I have known him for 13 months. He has always been a perfect gentleman in my presence. My wife also holds him in high esteem. He has visited my house continuously for the past 12 months. I certainly don't believe he has any connection with the case. If I thought for one minute that he is guilty," Rymer continued, "I would be one of the first to help the police convict him."[183]

"He opened my store at 8:30 every morning during the week of the homicide, and stayed there until 11 a.m. when I came down. He opened the store Thursday morning (the morning of the slaying) and called me on the telephone to tell me he was there and not to bother to hurry down. While there he signed several dated collection slips of which I have copies in the store. He was absolutely normal and sober at 11 a.m. Thursday when I came down to the store," Rymer asserted.[184]

Rymer was certain that the witnesses placing Wollner out and about Asheville the evening of and morning after the murder were simply confused about the date.


SHERIFF'S DEPUTIES SEARCHED WOLLNER'S studio and the home of Essie and Mildred Ward. They dug up a number of places in the Wards' yard but found nothing of interest. Inside the house they examined an ice pick and a pair of scissors.[185]

The investigators were looking for anything that might have made the gashes in Helen's face. At the Battery Park they had located a blood-stained ten-inch, nickel-plated letter opener in hotel manager Pat Branch's office. When presented in an evidence bag to the coroner, Dr. George F. Baier, he replied, "This is just the instrument I've been looking for."[186]

Two spots of blood were found on the paper knife—one near the end of the blade and another on the handle. For his part, Branch denied that the implement could have been used in the crime as it had been in his office for nearly four years and the bloodstains had probably been there for months, possibly caused by someone pricking their finger with the sharp blade.[187]

About the same time, in an alleyway just off Cherry Street, about a block and a half from the Battery Park Hotel, along a route in the direction the unknown man had fled, an unnamed woman found a pair of scissors. Thinking they were mistakenly thrown away by a resident at her home, she washed the scissors and tried to return them. When the suspected owner

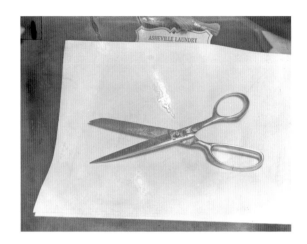

Pair of scissors found discarded near the hotel, 1936. *E.M. Ball Photographic Collection, D.H. Ramsey Library, Special Collections, UNC–Asheville, 28804.*

told her the scissors were not theirs, the woman immediately took the implement to the police station. The police then performed a benzidine test on the scissors, which came back positive for blood on the blades, though the coroner told the press that benzidine will show a "blood reaction" even with bloodstains that are several years old. The scissors were bagged as evidence.[188]

Investigators were particularly interested in the scissors because Dr. Baier found in his autopsy that Helen's right thumb was bruised and discolored—a defensive wound, the coroner concluded. "I noticed the thumb bruises when I examined the body. Her thumb apparently had been twisted as if she had picked up an instrument such as a pair of scissors to defend herself, and her assailant had jammed the point of the weapon into her face as she held it."[189]

THOUGH THE SEARCH OF Wollner's home and office turned up nothing to definitively tie him to the crime, Sheriff Brown continued to hold the musician on the fifteenth floor of the county courthouse, the only prisoner in that cell tier.

During Brown's daily press briefing, reporters peppered him with questions about Wollner. Brown gave his typically vague and stoic responses.

"Has he asked for an attorney?" one reporter queried.

"No."

"Has he been sleeping well?"

"Fair."

"Does he smoke much?"

"Yes, cigarettes."

"Has he any money?"

"Very little."

"Are friends permitted to see him?"

"No."

"Is he nervous?"

"Yes."

"Do you give him papers to read?"

"No, only magazines," the sheriff said, concluding the interview and walking away.[190]

Without access to the daily paper and cut off from contact with everyone except the jailor, Wollner impatiently waited in his cell for news about the investigation, pacing and flipping through magazines to pass the time until officers were ready to question him again.[191] Though the details of their second conversation were not released to the public, Sheriff Brown did tell the press that though Wollner changed his statement that evening, "he didn't change it very much about where he was," apparently reiterating that he was home all night.[192]

Over in the matron's quarters, Mildred Ward was also questioned again, but—like with Wollner—officers discovered "nothing new, nothing of interest."[193]

Rymer continued to try to see his friend. Finally, on Tuesday, though they were not allowed to talk about the murder or his alibi, Sheriff Brown allowed Rymer to speak briefly with Wollner and see how he was doing. Wollner's one request was that Rymer retrieve his violin from his studio for safe keeping. Rymer did one better than that. He delivered the $5,000 instrument to the jail the following day.[194]

And in the *Asheville Citizen*, a welcome sidebar graced the front page, surrounded by the gruesome coverage of Helen's murder. It read, "Classical music played by the skilled hand of a German born music master flooded through the cells and corridors of the Buncombe county jail for the first time last night as Mark Wollner...played his violin for more than half an hour....Inmates of the county prison, within hearing distance of Wollner's cell apparently were unmoved by the music that many persons in all parts of this country and Europe have paid to listen to. There was neither applause or objection when the violinist had concluded his musical program."[195]

But despite his ability to practice his craft, Wollner still seemed "discontented," according to the jailor. The violinist made no attempt to speak except to say, "I wonder why I am in here?" and immediately provide his own answer, "I guess it's just because I am a musician."[196]

W.H. Rymer delivers Mark Wollner's violin to the jailor, Guy Roberts, July 23, 1936.
*Associated Press photo, author's collection.*

As news of Wollner's despondent mood spread, friends, fans and his students began bringing tokens to the jail. And though they were not allowed to see him or send him notes, by the end of the day Wednesday, Wollner had received a large bouquet of red roses, a stack of magazines, an apple turnover and some ice cream, a bag of sandwiches and a half pint of wine (the sheriff would not allow the wine into the jail) and a bunch of gladioli. The gladioli were delivered by a ten-year-old student of Wollner's. The boy remarked after dropping off the flowers with the sheriff's office, "I believe he is innocent, but if he is guilty, I want him to pay."[197]

Public opinion on Wollner's guilt swung back and forth as new information was published and rumors circulated. While Wollner sat in jail, the clothes he had been wearing when he was arrested were in transit to the state laboratory in Raleigh for forensic investigation of several stains that looked like blood.[198]

BACK IN ASHEVILLE, THE chief of city detectives, Captain Fred Jones, asserted his belief that Wollner was innocent. "It looks to me like an inside job," he told reporters. "The man that did this job must be placed in the hotel by an eye-witness. I still have an open mind in the case, but it seems obvious to me that the murderer must have known the hotel thoroughly."[199]

What Jones did not tell reporters that day was that police were currently carrying out a careful investigation of the witnesses who had placed Wollner around town the night of the murder, and they were beginning to believe that they were all mistaken.[200]

"How is that?" asked Sheriff Brown of police chief Everett.

"I mean that we questioned all of the witnesses who saw Wollner, and they admit they confused Wednesday night with Thursday night. Now, if Mildred Ward admits Wollner came in early Friday morning, then that will just about prove the confusion of those witnesses, won't it?"

"I guess you're right," replied the sheriff. "Let's question Mildred again."

Asheville City Police detective Robert Patton inspects a coat taken from a suspect, July 1936. *E.M. Ball Photographic Collection, D.H. Ramsey Library Special Collections, UNC–Asheville, 28804.*

*Left*: Mildred Ward arrives at the sheriff's office, July 20, 1936. *Associated Press photo, author's collection.*

*Below*: W.H. Rymer and Mark Wollner (*right*) celebrate Wollner's release from jail at Rymer's home in Asheville, 1936. *E.M. Ball Photographic Collection, D.H. Ramsey Library Special Collections, UNC–Asheville, 28804.*

*Opposite*: Letter from Sheriff Brown to the state food and oil chemist, W.M. Allen, August 4, 1936. *Laurence Brown Collection, Swannanoa Valley Museum & History Center, Black Mountain, North Carolina.*

---

August 4, 1936.

Mr. W. M. Allen,
Raleigh, N. C.

Dear Sir:

      We sent you a piece of carpet with blood on it.
Please test this for type of blood. We will be glad if you
will return the clothes sent you at the same time, as the
owner of them has been released from investigation in this
crime.

      Please send the report of this examination of blood
stains to me.

                 Yours very truly,

                     L. E. Brown, Sheriff
                     Buncombe County.

LEB:C

---

Mildred, still in the matron's quarters, stood up when the men entered the room. They hurriedly asked whether Wollner had been out all night any time during the week of the murder.

"Yes," she said. "Mark stayed out all night Thursday."

"What time did he come in?"

"As nearly as I can remember, about 6 o'clock Friday morning. I talked with him."

"Then you still maintain Mark was at home all of Wednesday night?'

"Certainly," she quietly told the investigators.[201]

To be sure, the deputies backtracked and reinterviewed all of the witnesses who had incriminated Wollner by indicating that they saw him around Asheville late Wednesday night and early Thursday morning. All apparently admitted that perhaps they were mistaken—it must have been late Thursday night and early Friday morning that they saw him.[202]

Now convinced of Wollner's innocence, Brown ordered Mark and Mildred released from the jail. Wollner's clothes were returned to him from the state chemist without being analyzed.[203]

Overjoyed at the news of his friend's release, Rymer rushed to the jail with a clean shirt in hand. The following evening, Wollner's friends, colleagues and the press gathered at the Rymer home to celebrate.

As he laughed and joked with friends, Wollner proclaimed, "The good old U.S.A. is good enough for me" after Rymer suggested that perhaps they should plan a trip to Germany. Before the evening ended, Wollner stood in the parlor in his shirtsleeves and made a prepared statement to the press. He said, "I was a victim of circumstances and was confident that I was such a good musician that my professional reputation would not be damaged....I have lived through a Cuban revolution without carrying a gun, having nothing but my hands and my violin."[204]

# 4

# I DON'T KNOW WHY
# I FAILED TO PUNCH IT.

Feeling mounting pressure from the public, the press and Helen's family to solve the case, Sheriff Brown and his deputies drove back to the Battery Park Hotel to scour Helen's room for clues yet again, hoping to find some piece of physical evidence that would lead them to the perpetrator. The second floor was still off-limits to the public, and the hall was empty when Brown exited the elevator and turned the corner toward Helen's room. But before he could enter 224, the watch clock at the end of the hall caught his eye.

Daniel Gaddy, the watchman on duty the night of the murder, would have punched a key in the clock—as well as the clocks on every other floor of the hotel—on the hour, every hour, during his nightly rounds. The key made imprints on a paper disc installed in the clock and assured management that their security staff was doing their job.

"I guess Gaddy punched this and left before the murderer went to the girl's room," Sheriff Brown remarked to his deputies as they inspected the second-floor clock, only ten feet from Helen's door.[205]

The deputies lamented that if only Gaddy had done his rounds a little later during those early hours, perhaps he would have heard the disturbance and been able to come to Helen's aid. As it was, it seemed Gaddy had been on the elevator coming down from the roof when Helen's killer made his escape down the stairs and over the hotel's balustrade.

Somewhat absently, Sheriff Brown opened the clock to check the time intervals Gaddy had punched, hoping for a clearer picture of where the

A diagram of the second floor of the Battery Park Hotel noting the guests occupying each room the night of the murder. The night watchman's clock is just outside room 223. *Asheville Citizen, August 2, 1936.*

murderer might have been as Gaddy made his rounds. But as the metal door swung open, Sheriff Brown and his deputies looked at the clock in near disbelief. The paper disc at the time of the murder was blank.

"Cover every floor and examine every clock," Brown barked at his deputies, immediately aware of the potential importance of this revelation. "See if any other has not been punched—and don't skip any."

The deputies climbed floor to floor, examining each clock carefully. Gaddy had inserted the brass key into the clocks every hour on every floor during his shifts the entire week, except the hour between 1:00 a.m. and 2:00 a.m. the night of the murder.[206] On further inspection, investigators found that this was the only time over the last month that the night watchman had failed to punch the clock while on duty at the hotel.[207]

Officers immediately picked Gaddy up, brought him to the county jail and deposited him in the office of the high sheriff for questioning.[208]

DANIEL HENRY GADDY, THE white twenty-eight-year-old son of a dairy farmer turned prison guard, was a new father. His son, Daniel Jr., would turn two in less than a month.[209] "Stickily-built [and] almost bald,"[210] Gaddy had previously worked as a cab driver before being hired at Battery Park as the night watchman. Having attended school only through the sixth grade, he had been working to make his own living since he turned fourteen. This job was a step up for him and a boon for his family. Gaddy and his wife, Sue, rented a "shabby, second floor apartment" in Asheville, also making room for Sue's father, brother and sister.[211]

"He never took a drink in his life and never did anything wrong," Gaddy's father said of his son after the arrest.[212]

Gaddy, who appeared shocked to be in custody, "turned waxen and pale" as he entered the sheriff's office.[213]

"Why did you not punch your clock on the second floor at one o'clock?" Sheriff Brown asked as Gaddy carefully took a seat in the chair opposite him.

"I did," Gaddy asserted, "his lips twitch[ing] nervously. 'I punched them all just as usual.'"[214]

When the sheriff slid the blank paper disc toward him, Gaddy fell silent. The sheriff waited. Finally, breaking the silence, Gaddy ventured a guess that perhaps the clock had failed to register the punch; the timing was just a coincidence.[215]

"Have you your key ring with you?" Brown asked.

"Yes, here it is," Gaddy said, handing him the keys from his belt.

Everyone in the room sat in rapt silence as Brown examined the ring, key by key. Choosing one, he leaned toward Gaddy and held it out to him saying, "This key will open 224, won't it?"

Gaddy nodded.

"You see it's partly broken, don't you?"

"Well, I damaged it while trying to get into a vacant house I was thinking about renting on Bartlett Street," Gaddy offered.[216]

Gaddy may not have immediately known why Sheriff Brown was interested in the broken key, but the deputies in the room certainly did. When

*Above*: Daniel Gaddy with his wife, Sue, and son, Daniel Jr., 1936. *ACME photograph, author's collection.*

*Opposite*: The door to room 224 showing the button that indicates if the door is locked, 1936. *E.M. Ball Photographic Collection, D.H. Ramsey Library Special Collections, UNC–Asheville, 28804.*

officers arrived at the crime scene, they found a key in the exterior lock on Helen's door. Though neither William Clevenger nor the hotel carpenter, Henry Laetsche, could recall a key being in the door when they discovered Helen's body, Deputy Brown had marked the key as evidence but had not immediately followed up.[217]

A few days later, Sheriff Brown took it on himself to see if this mysterious key might lead anywhere.

"I tried the key in the lock [to Helen's room]," Brown recalled. "To my amazement, I discovered that it was what is called a 'master key' and was capable of unlocking from the outside a door which a guest had locked from the inside, with the inside key still in the door." Other reports, however, quoted manager Branch as saying that if the door was locked from the inside it could only be opened from the outside by an "emergency pass key." There was only one of these keys in existence. It belonged to Branch and it had not been out of his possession.[218]

Either way, when a door was locked from the inside, a small button between the knob and the keyhole protruded from the brass plate, which allowed the hall maid to know that the room was occupied. While the hall maid's key would unlock the door only if the door was not locked from the inside, a key like the one found inside the exterior lock the morning of the murder would throw the bolt even if Helen had engaged the interior lock.

Realizing that it was very likely that he held the key to the murderer's identity, Sheriff Brown at once tracked down Edwin D. Frady, the chief engineer at the hotel, to find out which of the employees had been issued a master key and who might no longer be in possession of their key.[219]

But if Brown expected a speedy solution to the crime based on the key, he was sorely disappointed.

"Eleven keys were issued to 11 persons on the hotel staff," Brown told reporters. "We talked to all of these persons and had them produce their keys. The master key found in the door was a 12th key, but it may have been one of the original 11."

"Do you have any explanation of the 12th key?" shouted a member of the press.

"No," he answered.

"Is there any question in your mind that the skeleton key found in the lock was used by the killer?"

"None at all."

"Is the report true that Gaddy's skeleton key found on his key ring is too badly broken to work in a lock?"[220]

"Yes. Apparently Gaddy did not frequently find use for his pass key."[221]

Sheriff Brown sent his deputies down to the Bartlett Street house where Gaddy said he had broken his copy of the master key. They removed the door lock and extracted a small L-shaped bit of steel that fit the broken portion of Gaddy's key exactly.[222]

According to Frady, there were only eleven keys. Yet on comparison with the other master keys, this twelfth key did appear to have also been made by Frady. But no one at the hotel, neither Frady who issued the keys nor Pat Branch, the manager,[223] could tell Brown how there came to be twelve keys or to whom the key might have belonged.

Despite being unable to tie the key to any one person, discovering that it was a master key shifted the investigation efforts toward people who had the easiest access to a master key—the employees.

Sheriff Brown took several of his deputies and two stenographers and began gathering written statements. Each employee was brought up to a room near the rooftop garden at the hotel and asked to share anything they knew that might help unveil the perpetrator.

Evelyn Moss, who was the only other person on the second-floor hallway besides Henry Laeschte when William Clevenger found his niece's

Evelyn Moss, maid at the Battery Park Hotel, 1936. *E.M. Ball Photographic Collection, D.H. Ramsey Library Special Collections, UNC–Asheville, 28804.*

body, sat down for her first interview with officers. Moss, "an unusually intelligent maid"[224] according to Sheriff Brown, had been completing her routine check of the floor prior to William Clevenger's arrival in the hallway the morning of the murder. As part of her duties, she would write down whether a room was occupied or unoccupied, which she determined by noting the position of the small button protruding from between the brass knob and the keyhole. If the door was locked from the inside—and presumably occupied—then the button would be out. If the button was in, then Moss marked the room as unoccupied.[225]

Moss told detectives—and showed them the paperwork—that the button on Helen's door had been protruding at 8:20 a.m. when she did her inspection, indicating that the door was locked from the inside. She had also recorded William Clevenger's door as being locked that morning prior to his arrival at Helen's room.[226]

Just ten minutes later, however, William Clevenger found Helen's door unlocked. Sheriff Brown began to wonder. Did that mean that the murderer was still inside the room at 8:20? Was the mysterious intruder seen vaulting the balustrade around 1:00 a.m. just an odd coincidence?[227]

Though Brown investigated this angle and reporters speculated wildly, Brown eventually found that the button on the lock would protrude as long as the key was in the interior lock, and the key could be in the lock without the bolt being thrown. So, it was very possible that Helen's door had been unlocked since at least the time of the murder, if not the entire night. Helen's bloodstained key, however, was later found under the radiator against the far wall. Investigators made no mention of how it might have gotten there.[228]

The mystery of the twelfth key persisted. Despite its pervasiveness in newspaper reports, as the investigation dragged on, Sheriff Brown concluded, "Frankly, I think it was left there by a maid or another employee following discovery of the crime. Afterward this person refused to admit having left the key there. Although no one claims ownership and all 11 previously issued have been traced. I'm not going to attach too much importance unless I have to."[229]

BUT FOR NOW, THE key was still a vital clue in the sheriff's mind. Brown and his deputies continued to question Gaddy, who remained adamant that he had no knowledge of who had killed Helen.

Having exhausted his lines of questioning but still feeling as though Gaddy knew more than he was saying and could perhaps even be the solution to the whole case, Sheriff Brown called the jailer to walk Gaddy up to the fifteenth floor of the courthouse and close him in a cell alone, isolated from other prisoners.[230]

"Working on the idea that when he got ready to talk he would send for me," Brown said, "I left him strictly alone, but I received reports every few hours....All of these tended to bear out my idea that Gaddy, for some reason we could not figure, was a badly scared man."[231]

Though Gaddy had not been charged with any crime, by law Sheriff Brown was allowed to hold him as long as he wanted or until Gaddy demanded a habeas corpus hearing, in which a judge would determine whether he could continue to be held without charges being filed.[232]

Gaddy spent several more nights in jail. Scared and feeling as though he "was being unjustly held,"[233] Gaddy refused the meals the jailer offered him, instead eating out of a large box of sandwiches from a friend and drinking milk his wife had sent.[234]

Gaddy paced the cell but, eventually, worn out, sat on his bunk, his face in his hands, seemingly absorbed in his thoughts. The magazines given to him to help pass the time went unread.[235]

Buncombe County Courthouse, 1930s. *E.M. Ball Photographic Collection, D.H. Ramsey Library Special Collections, UNC–Asheville, 28804.*

"He is almost ready to jump out of his skin," a man who visited Gaddy said.[236]

"I believe Gaddy is going to tell me something tomorrow. I really believe it," the sheriff told the reporters camped outside his office that evening. "I believe the key to the whole situation is Gaddy." Turning to leave, the sheriff muttered, "The solution to this thing is in the hotel. It's right there."[237]

Gaddy's wife attempted to visit her husband in jail several times. She was not allowed to see him. Like others involved in the case, even tangentially, Sue Gaddy was peppered with questions from reporters as she made her way from the courthouse.[238]

Sue held strong. She was certain her husband was not only "innocent of all charges"[239] but also that he had already told the sheriff all he knew about what had happened the night of Helen's murder. Still, she feared engaging a lawyer for Gaddy might "aggravate" his situation and make it look as though he really was guilty of some crime.[240]

"I know my husband don't know anything more than he's told them. They think he does, but I know he don't. He ain't that kind of a man," Sue told one reporter.[241]

Gaddy's sixty-year-old father, Henry, however, was not as confident in his son as Sue was in her husband. He sent a letter to the jail, pleading with his son to "tell the truth."[242]

Perhaps his father's letter did the trick, or maybe Gaddy simply got his fill of life alone in a jail cell, but on July 23, the same day Gaddy received the missive from his father, Sheriff Brown coyly told reporters that Gaddy's memory was now "much better," though Brown refused to elaborate.[243]

Another member of the sheriff's department, however, was not as tight-lipped. Apparently, Gaddy had finally admitted that he knew he had forgotten to punch the watch clock.[244]

"I don't know why I failed to punch it," Gaddy told Brown. "I have been worrying a great deal about financial matters. I guess I simply overlooked it."

"You realize that sounds mighty weak," the sheriff replied.

"Yes, I do. I just can't understand why I failed to punch it. I saw the door to room 218 open and that worried me. After investigating that I suppose I must have thought I already had punched the clock when I didn't."[245] He continued to tell Sheriff Brown that his wife was ill and that he was worrying over making payments on his automobile.[246]

But Sheriff Brown was still not satisfied. "Gaddy knows something and I think he is getting ready to talk. When he talks we'll be able to break the case."[247] He sent Gaddy back to his cell.[248]

Though the hotel's executive staff spoke unflaggingly of Gaddy's innocence and good character, the hotel offered Gaddy's wife and young son no assistance, financial or otherwise. In explanation, Pat Branch said, "The management [is] in a peculiar situation. If [we] assist Mr. Gaddy's family during his stay in jail, it might [be] construed as covering up or protecting someone. However, we [don't] feel that Gaddy [is] at fault."[249]

A new night watchman, a former city police officer, took over Gaddy's duties.[250]

Daniel Gaddy sits in his jail cell, July 21, 1936. *Associated Press photograph, author's collection.*

NEWS OF GADDY'S DEMEANOR and activities in the jail filtered out to reporters. He was "downcast," he had been talking little, he was sleeping well, he had stopped shaving, he did not like the jail food but was eating regularly thanks to food and drink sent in daily by friends and family.[251]

At the end of July, Gaddy's father decided that his son had spent enough time behind bars and began looking for a lawyer. "I think he's been there long enough with nothing charged against him," Henry Gaddy told reporters and indicated that he had obtained the services of John C. Cheesborough, solicitor of the general county court.

"We hope to get him out tomorrow," the elder Gaddy continued.

Cheesborough, however, denied he had been hired by the Gaddys; rather, he said he merely told Henry Gaddy that he would speak with Sheriff Brown about releasing Gaddy "as soon as he conveniently" could.[252]

Sheriff Brown did allow one concession—Henry Gaddy could visit his son for a few minutes, under supervision by Brown himself.

On leaving the courthouse, Henry Gaddy said his son was in good spirits but that the family was no longer "making any effort to have the boy released from jail."[253]

Sheriff Brown questioned Gaddy daily but learned nothing new. Still, Brown told reporters, "I'm going to hold him until I'm sure he can't do me any more good."[254]

# 5

# I WILL STAY HERE IN JAIL 'TIL DOOMSDAY.

O n the evening of July 18, Helen left Asheville for the final time.[255] Lying inside a wooden casket, a small bouquet of greenery tied with a ribbon on top, Helen traveled in the baggage car of a train headed to her father's hometown, Fletcher, Ohio, alongside canvas bags of mail, paper-wrapped parcels and steamer trunks. Beside her coffin was a child-sized ladder-back chair, lying on its side.[256]

Joseph and William Clevenger, too, began the more than 450-mile trip north for Helen's funeral and burial[257] despite Sheriff Brown's desire to detain William for questioning.[258]

"He assured me that he would come back through Asheville on his way to Raleigh and assist me in any way that he could," the sheriff said in response to quiet rumblings among Asheville residents about the departure from the city of one of their prime suspects in Helen's murder.[259]

The Clevenger brothers were not the only ones making the trek to the small Ohio town, which would be Helen's final resting place. Several hundred curious spectators filtered into Fletcher on the day of Helen's funeral, hoping to catch a glimpse of the now-famous victim and her family. Many people, mostly women, had already attempted to view Helen's body at the Norland-Brown Funeral Home in Asheville. All requests had been declined.[260]

Though little about Helen's funeral made the newspaper in Asheville, the *Piqua Daily Call* out of Ohio reported:

*No trace of the horror and terror preceding her tragic death by the hands of a brutal murderer marred the calm serenity of Helen Clevenger's face as her body lay in state at the Suber Funeral Parlor, awaiting burial today beside members of her family. The quiet street outside the funeral parlor and the calm within so completely denied the incredible crime. Golden-haired and short in stature, the murdered girl looked younger than her 19 years. Gashes on her face, one of which beside the nose had penetrated as far as the palate, had been skillfully hidden.*[261]

The paper also reported that the Clevenger family were Methodists, but in actuality, Helen and her parents were followers of the Baha'i faith, which the *Asheville Citizen* reported to its readers as being "a religion that teaches the spiritual unity of mankind advocating universal peace."[262] The *San Francisco Examiner* later wrote that Helen's death could be blamed in part on the young woman's faith in the "occult religion which teaches among other things that

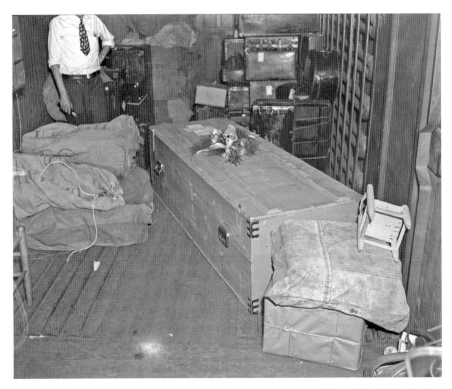

Helen's casket traveling in a boxcar to Ohio, 1936. *Associated Press photograph, author's collection.*

Helen Clevenger's headstone. *Findagrave.com.*

Helen's father, Joseph, and Helen's aunts and uncles watch as Helen's casket is lowered into her grave. (*Front row, from left to right*): Harley Clevenger, Joseph Clevenger, Mellie Clevenger, William Clevenger and Elizabeth Clevenger, Fletcher, Ohio, July 22, 1936. *ACME Newspictures, author's collection.*

the world should be trusted, and that doors [like that of her hotel room] should not be locked against one's fellow-men."[263] The Baha'i symbol for God was etched at the top of Helen's granite gravestone between the years of her birth and death.[264]

After the "simple, private service"[265] in the funeral home's chapel, which was "barred to everyone except about 75 relatives and close friends,"[266] Helen's body was transported to Fletcher Cemetery, her casket draped with a gray cloth and almost obscured by a large bouquet of greenery and flowers.

A small crowd followed the hearse to the gravesite. Her father and uncles removed their hats and stood with their hands clasped on the front row watching stoically as Helen's casket dropped slowly into the dark earth, not far from the small headstones of her only siblings, who had both died as infants. Helen's mother had been too unwell to make the trip from New York to attend the burial of her last living child.[267]

BACK IN ASHEVILLE, SHERIFF Brown was feeling increasing public pressure.

"I have five more months in office," Brown said as the investigation dragged on, "and I am fairly sure of re-election for another two-year term. I am willing, and I am determined to subordinate all else to a solution for this mystery, for all that time if it is necessary."[268]

So he began an effort anew to interview the hotel's employees. After finishing up his fifty-eighth interview of the day, he made his way to street level, where he met the throng of reporters gathered outside his office on the east side of the courthouse. "I found some very interesting facts," he told them.

"Did you find anything that might point to the solution of the crime?" one reporter queried.

"Yes."

"Is there any estimate on when the case will be solved?" another shouted over the crowd.

"I'll say that I'll make another arrest within two days."

"Will he be the murderer?"

"I didn't say that. I expect to arrest the criminal in a couple of days."

"The criminal or the murderer?" a reporter asked for clarification.

"Call him the criminal, the murderer, or anything you want," Brown said, concluding the interview.[269]

This statement to the press started a countdown. The public was now sure that Sheriff Brown would arrest the murderer in forty-eight hours, about the same time that Helen's uncle was set to arrive back in Asheville.

But the sheriff soon became agitated when he found out that William was driving north to his brother's Staten Island home. Brown quickly began making phone calls, finally tracking the brothers down in Kentucky and demanding that William come back to Asheville at once. William turned his car south; Joseph caught a train to New York.[270]

Sensing the court of public opinion turning on William, the Pegrams came to his defense. Mrs. Pegram told the press that William had not only started a college fund for Helen but had also started bank accounts for her own four daughters as well.[271] And just a few hours before the murder, Mrs. Pegram recalled sitting with William, making small talk. He mentioned that the women he worked with had recommended the Battery Park Hotel as a safe place for Helen to stay. He was very protective of the girl, she explained.[272]

Mrs. Pegram made it clear that when William arrived back in Asheville, he had an open invitation "to stop at the Pegram home."[273]

So, before making his way back to the city, William drove to the Pegrams and called Sheriff Brown. Brown instructed William to come to his office immediately but told him to use the public elevators located directly through

A crowd gathers outside the sheriff's office, July 25, 1936. *E.M. Ball Photographic Collection, D.H. Ramsey Library Special Collections, UNC–Asheville, 28804.*

the front doors of the courthouse so that he could avoid the "curious crowd and the small army of newspaper men collected in and about [the sheriff's] office"[274] at the back of the courthouse, waiting for the sheriff to make his promised arrest.

William took Brown's advice. The sheriff stood just outside the passenger elevators, impatient for the professor to arrive. When the elevator door finally slid open and William stepped out, Brown escorted him directly to the jailer's quarters to begin the interrogation.[275]

Clevenger took a seat across from the sheriff. He was "calm and determined,"[276] telling Brown quietly, "I'm not going to consider that I'm under arrest, but I will stay here in jail 'til doomsday if it will help you clear up this mystery."[277]

Brown questioned Clevenger for more than three hours. At the end of the interview, he explained, "I found Professor Clevenger ready to 'play ball' with me and this made my difficult tasks much easier. I had a talk with him, going over a second time the details that he could give me about his actions the night before and the morning after the murder. Then I went downstairs to where the newspaper men were waiting." [278]

BY THE FORTY-EIGHT-HOUR DEADLINE, which fell at 7:00 p.m., the crowd around the sheriff's office had grown to more than five hundred—and potentially as large as eight hundred—all waiting for the announcement that William Clevenger had been arrested for the murder of his niece.[279]

"Doctors, lawyers, and all professions were represented in the curious and interested onlookers," the *Asheville Citizen* reported.[280] Rumors spread through the crowd of "arrests, confessions, and suicide." The atmosphere was tense but rife with excitement as the deadline approached. Still, the window shades at the sheriff's office remained drawn.[281]

With reporters camped out on the floor awaiting the press conference, deputies began bringing chairs out into the hallway. The press waiting outside passed the time by "pitching pennies from the stone wall outside the sheriff's office to little negro boys on Davidson Street."[282]

While they waited, the reporters prepared a list of five questions among themselves, knowing that their time with the sheriff would be limited. The questions they hoped to ask were: Have you made an arrest? Who is it? With what is he charged? Is this the arrest you predicted? and Has he confessed?[283]

The clock struck the hour. The sheriff's office door remained locked. "It's after seven. Where's the murderer?" came yells from the crowd.[284] Five minutes after 7:00 p.m., Brown appeared. He conferred with the county attorney for a few minutes before finally ushering the newspapermen—and one woman, a reporter from Washington, D.C.—to his office, the shades still drawn, and locked the door. The reporters crammed into the office, jostling for a position nearest the sheriff, while Brown seated himself in the chair behind his desk.

Ignoring their questions, he calmly read from notes he had jotted down in pencil.

"Professor Clevenger is being detained for questioning," the sheriff said. He told reporters that William was given quarters adjoining the jailer's room. "He is allowed full use of the jail and telephones," he added.

"I had hoped to have a confession for you boys at this time," Brown said. "I'm sorry I have to disappoint you, but it may be a week or 10 days before a confession can be released owing to new developments in the case."

"Do you call that an arrest?" one reporter asked of Professor Clevenger's detention at the jail.

"That's all I'm going to tell you about this thing," the sheriff replied, unlocking the door and ushering the reporters out of his office.[285]

Despite the lack of any new information, as soon as Brown finished his statement, the out-of-town reporters rushed to nearby telephones to call in what they had gleaned to their home offices. The crowd of onlookers remained long after Brown had left for his home in Black Mountain.[286] Professor Clevenger spent the night at the jail.

Coverage of the case continued to sell papers. Cars lined up outside the Asheville offices of the *Citizen* and the *Times*, waiting for the release of a new issue, mobbing the newspaper boy when he emerged carrying a stack.[287] The papers even reported on the public's insatiable interest in any bit of information related to the murder and investigation; the *Asheville Citizen* had an ongoing column called Bits of News Picked Up in Slaying Probe, noting any nuggets of information that could not fit in the larger front-page stories.

The *Asheville Citizen* reported:

> *Over tea cups, at the luncheon table, between bridge hands, in the beauty parlor, in offices, over telephones, and almost at every point during the day in Asheville there is some or much mention of the murder. All are anxious to learn what others think of the crime, and also to voice their own opinions of events leading to and following the slaying of the 18-year-old New York university student. Papers are rapidly devoured for fullest details concerning the progress of the investigation, and the public avidly follows*

*each movement of Sheriff Laurence Brown and his aides. The crime was even reported in Greek in a Greek newspaper illustrated with photographs, it was learned here yesterday.* The Citizen *and* The Times *are called numerous times during the day for information. Many long-distance calls on the subject have been received here.*[288]

And people did not stop with talking about the crime. Visitors and residents alike "want[ed] to see the place where the girl was slain and [drove] by the hotel with their necks craning from the cars. Numerous of the curious…visited the hotel veranda to see where the man who ran from the lobby leaped over the railing."[289] One resident, an "overall clad farmer," unbeknownst to him, entertained Battery Park guests for thirty minutes while he walked around the veranda, staring up at the top of the building and over the railing.[290]

BACK IN NEW YORK, Joseph Clevenger refused to speak to reporters. "He has gone to bed after returning from Helen's funeral and cannot be disturbed," the family's spokesman told the media.

"We knew Professor Clevenger would be detained," he added. "The move is merely in line with routine investigation. We are not upset about it."[291]

The following morning, Brown continued to question William Clevenger.

"I went over with Professor Clevenger a number of statements that we had taken from various witnesses in the case. I thought perhaps something

William Clevenger testifies at the coroner's inquest into his niece's death, Asheville, North Carolina, July 18, 1936. *Associated Press photograph, author's collection.*

in them would bring to his mind some forgotten point that would be of help to us," Brown said.[292]

At the end of the day, reporters caught the sheriff on his way to his car and began asking about the professor's whereabouts.

"He's still right here in this jail, like he was last night," Brown replied.

"Is he remaining here voluntarily?"

"It means the same thing."

"What if he tries to walk out, will you stop him?"

Confident, Brown replied, "He won't try to walk out. He wants to stay here to avoid curious people and photographers until his part of this thing is cleared up. And I want him here. He's helping to go over the statements of hotel employees to see if he can remember anything helpful."[293]


WHILE WILLIAM SPENT ANOTHER night behind a steel door, an entire corridor to himself,[294] investigators traveled to Raleigh to look into reports that the professor was a "peculiar person." They interviewed the professor's superiors, colleagues, friends and students.[295] At the same time, reporters in Raleigh were working a similar angle.

The fifty-two-year-old had been employed by the college for over a decade. He spent half his time teaching animal husbandry and dairying and the other half working with the agricultural extension service.[296]

One of the college staff members remarked to a reporter, "I feel like I hardly know him, you never found him mixing socially at all."[297] And several of his students said that they found William "a little peculiar."[298]

At the jail, William fretted about his future, hoping that the publicity related to the murder investigation would not lose him his job or reputation. He need not have worried. His friends and colleagues actively rushed to his defense. William's immediate supervisor and at least six other of his animal husbandry co-workers issued signed statements affirming their belief in his good character.[299]

The extension service director, Dean I.O. Schaub, who had known William even before he began working at the college, commented, "He is a fine fellow and a good teacher. He is held in highest regard. He seldom mixed much socially though he sometimes went to things like the faculty dances."

"Do you consider Clevenger eccentric?" a reporter asked.

"No, not eccentric or peculiar, just an old bachelor," Schaub explained. "His habits were fine. We never had heard of anything against him before—I

William Clevenger, 1939.
*University Archives Photograph Collection. People (UA023.024), Special Collections Research Center at NC State University Libraries.*

know he helped out people who were in need. He was considerate and I understand he was helping his niece through college."[300]

William's living situation also came under intense scrutiny. Officers conducted an exhaustive examination of the dormitory room at the college where William lived as part of his role as a faculty advisor. Described as plainly furnished "almost to the point of severity," William's room contained family photographs, including one of Helen, but no letters or mail, no gun or cartridges and no photographs of other young girls.[301] Two of the students who lived on the same floor as the professor, thought of him as a "big brother" and mentioned that he "was always in a jovial mood, even when in his capacity as faculty adviser... he was forced to reprimand students for making unnecessary noise."[302]

"He bore a fine reputation," Sheriff Brown said of William once the officers reported back to him on the results of their investigation. "This fitted in exactly with the impression I had gathered from talking to him," Brown concluded.[303]

TWO DAYS AFTER WILLIAM'S detention, as reporters stood outside the courthouse waiting for updates on the case, a messenger arrived with a telegram for the professor. A few minutes later, the boy returned, the crisp paper missive still unopened. He had been told that William was no longer in the jail. Reporters stormed inside, but the deputy on duty refused to confirm or deny whether the professor had indeed left.

Not to be deterred, a few reporters found William's brother Clinton and asked if the professor was still jailed.

"Well, the sheriff says so," Clinton replied.

"Have you seen him today?" one asked, referring to William.

"Yes."

"But you haven't visited the jail?"

"That's true," Clinton replied.

Later that afternoon, William's lawyer announced to reporters that William had left the jail and gone into seclusion "somewhere in

Asheville."[304] Unsurprisingly, the secret location was later revealed to be the Pegrams' home.[305]

This was all news to Sheriff Brown, who had taken the day off. When reporters tracked him down at his home to inquire, Brown replied, "He was there when I left last night. I don't think he would leave unless I told him to."

"Do you expect him to leave the jail soon?" one reporter asked.

Perhaps realizing that the reporters knew more than he did about William's whereabouts, Brown replied, "I don't want to say anything further about Clevenger."[306]

Not long afterward, Sheriff Brown "thundered up the driveway behind the 15-story courthouse, cutting a leaping swath through a group of newspaper correspondents and smashing his own office door in a shatter of splinters. The sheriff leapt out [of his armor-plated automobile] and dashed for his office, slamming the door."[307]


MONDAY MORNING, WILLIAM DROVE into the city to speak first with Sheriff Brown and then with the press. William told Brown he would raise the funds to hire a private investigator to aid in solving the case, but when questioned by reporters at the rear of the courthouse, he "did not divulge the sheriff's feelings along this line."[308]

He told reporters once more, tears welling in his eyes, of finding Helen's body. "A man can't keep telling that over and…" he trailed off, choking up. Taking a breath and collecting himself, he told reporters of being escorted back to his room in a "daze" after finding Helen's body, assuming that the authorities were being notified.

The professor was critical of the hotel's response. "A more careful check should have been made to determine the cause of the disturbance," he explained. He insisted that he was sure his niece would have locked her door and so "whoever got to her did so with a pass key."[309]

Dismissing the theory that the murder could have been revenge for Helen's father's work as a "food and drug adulteration expert" for the U.S. Department of Agriculture—Joseph had "figured in some mighty big findings" related to impure foods and drugs[310]—William said he could only visualize the crime as one of passion, remarking that the one consolation he had was that his niece "died protecting her honor" by "put[ting] up a terrible struggle."[311]

"[I believe it was] an inside affair [and I] would not be surprised at any time to learn of the arrest of a man whose name so far has been mentioned in connection with the case only in rumor," William said. "In [my] own mind

William Clevenger speaks with reporters outside the Buncombe County Courthouse, July 27, 1936. *E.M. Ball Photographic Collection, D.H. Ramsey Library Special Collections, UNC–Asheville, 28804.*

[I have] a definite idea about the identity of the culprit." He was particularly alarmed that he was forced back into his room while the hotel manager and other employees went in and out of Helen's room—and that they did so for an hour before calling the authorities.[312] With misty eyes, he lamented, "She would have been going home this week."[313]

Now "temporarily eliminated" as a suspect, Professor Clevenger left Asheville with the promise that he would come back if "anything turned up to complicate the case."[314] Though at the time the sheriff did not reveal why he had been so determined to hold William, Brown's deputies later recalled that "Clevenger insisted, over and over, that he never kissed or fondled his niece, and that always he took a room far removed from hers. Clevenger repeated this so often that Sheriff Brown's suspicions were aroused to the point of wanting to check up on the Professor minutely."[315]

As to the man mentioned "only in rumor," little else was said beyond a single paragraph tacked onto the end of a long article in an interior page of the *Asheville Citizen*. The final paragraph of the story, which was primarily about William leaving the jail, read, "Widespread rumors that the son of a prominent Asheville business man had been taken into custody in connection with the murder and was being held in jail in Raleigh for safekeeping were spiked last night by announcements by Sheriff Brown and the father of the youth who said there was no basis for the report. Just how the rumor started is not known but it had gained wide circulation."[316] The youth was not named.

That same day, an Asheville man was arrested on disorderly conduct charges in Charleston, South Carolina. As he was placed in a cell, he yelled, "You'd give a lot of money to know what I know about Asheville." When he sobered up, the officers questioned him about Helen's murder. He replied, "I was so drunk I didn't know what I was saying. I must have been just acting big. I surely don't want to get mixed up in nothing like that."[317] Though neither the papers nor the public wanted to go on the record identifying rumored suspects by name, they were all certainly talking among themselves.

# 6

# IT'S WHAT I'SE WONDERIN', TOO!

Despite an intense search for an additional murder weapon beyond a .32-caliber automatic pistol, investigators began to suspect that the gashes in Helen's face could have been made by a ridge on the clip of the gun.[318]

"It is not logical that a killer would have carried two deadly weapons with him to that room, switching from one to the other," Sheriff Brown told reporters.[319] The normally tight-lipped Brown continued to explain,

> *I think that in all probability the automatic fired one shot, the shell that was in the chamber, and then jammed without throwing a second cartridge into the chamber. The murderer, in a frantic effort to silence his victim and get out of the room, turned the gun into a club and pounded Miss Clevenger in the face as she lay dying from the mortal wound inflicted by the bullet. The cartridge clip on a gun of that type would have made the small crescent-shaped wounds seen on Miss Clevenger's face, while the weight of the weapon, in the case of the heavier blows, could easily have made the larger, and more ragged cuts.[320]*

By dismissing the many implements—scissors, a paper knife and even a can opener—that had previously been thought to have made the gashes in Helen's face, and centering on the pistol, finding the .32-caliber German- or Spanish-type automatic grew increasingly important in solving the case.[321] The investigators "ripped up carpets, tore out ventilating grilles, searched storage closets and fire hose receptacles, even sifted sand in hotel cuspidors; and found nothing."[322]

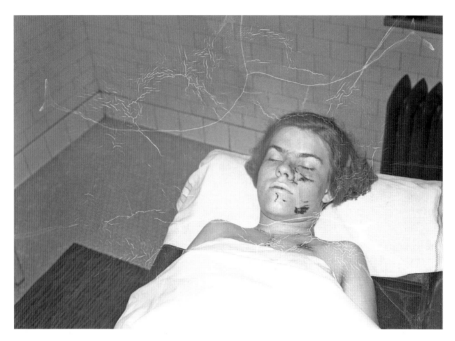

Helen Clevenger at Noland-Brown Funeral Home, July 1936. *E.M. Ball Photographic Collection, D.H. Ramsey Library Special Collections, UNC–Asheville, 28804.*

Without the pistol, the most promising physical evidence was the bullet pulled from Helen's body and one empty shell found in her hotel bathroom. The shell was stamped with an uppercase *H* and three stars.[323] Detectives were unfamiliar with these markings." After checking every store in the area, the investigators told reporters from the *Citizen* that no similar bullets with those particular markings had been sold in Asheville for the past ten years. A reporter out of New Jersey, however, wrote that Sheriff Brown had told him that the bullet and shell had been traced to a local army supply store, which had acquired the ammunition from a "defunct hardware company." Because the bullet was no longer being manufactured, Sheriff Brown labeled it an "outlaw" brand.[324]

Perhaps hoping to reap the monetary reward that had grown to $1,000 for information that would lead to the "arrest, delivery, and conviction"[325] of the person responsible for Helen's death, tipsters began funneling information to the sheriff about hotel employees who might own a gun.[326]

At Battery Park, an unnamed Black employee whispered to the officers that "before the murder…he had been puzzled by the fact that L.D. Roddy, elevator operator, had taken Edward Fleming, bellboy, to the second floor on two trips." When the pair returned to the lobby much later, Fleming was seen carrying a bundle of clothes under his arm, which he quickly left the hotel with. After hearing this report, deputies immediately went to detain Roddy and Fleming, both of whom were Black.[327]

James Edward Fleming, a twenty-five-year-old father, was arrested without incident at his Flint Street home and taken to the jail for questioning.[328] He repeatedly denied having traveled with Roddy to the second floor or anywhere in the vicinity of Helen's room. Detectives felt certain that Fleming was lying and sent him to a cell for the night.[329]

The following afternoon, Fleming asked the jailor if he could speak with Sheriff Brown. Brown came immediately.

"What do you have to say, Fleming?" the sheriff asked him through the bars.

"Sheriff, I lied about not going to that second floor," Fleming said. "I did go, but I went up there when the girl was on her first trip here, and she was on the third floor then."

Coroner George F. Baier Jr. examines the bullet that killed Helen and its casing, 1936. *E.M. Ball Photographic Collection, D.H. Ramsey Library Special Collections, UNC–Asheville, 28804.*

"What did you go up on the second floor for?" Brown replied.

"To get some suits to have cleaned and pressed for one of the guests. I took them to the cleaners myself. You can find out the truth of that by asking them over at the cleaners," Fleming explained.

Brown nodded and left Fleming to wait.[330]

Brown went back to his office to confer with his deputies. "And I really believe he's telling the truth," Brown told them. "Nevertheless, Tom, you and Love [Gudger] check the cleaners and the guest registration on the girl's first trip, before she checked out. Tie them up and see if the pieces fit."

Several hours later, the deputies had confirmed Fleming's story—the mysterious visits to the second floor, in fact to room 224, had occurred during Helen's first visit to the hotel, while Helen was in her room on the third floor. The cleaners had record of Fleming dropping off two suits to be pressed that morning and picking them up a little over an hour later.[331]

Fleming was released later that day. When asked why he refused to explain the mix-up when he was first arrested, he replied that he was "too scared" to let the deputies know that he had been to room 224, even though Helen had not been staying in it at the time.[332] Despite—or perhaps because of—this fear, in 1947, he began training at the local police school. The following year, he became a junior patrolman with the "Negro section of the city police department"—only the third Black police officer the city had hired. Fleming retired in 1978 as a sergeant.[333]

Lem D. Roddy Jr. was a little trickier for officers to pin down. When deputies arrived at his home on Hill Street at 10:00 p.m., around the same time they were detaining Fleming nearby, Roddy "ran out the rear and down into a valley" to avoid officers.[334]

About five hours later, they were able to track down the twenty-six-year-old married father of two at the Battery Park Hotel and bring him to the county jail, where they questioned him for twenty minutes about his movements the night of the murder.

"The sheriff asked me what I did after I got off work that night," Roddy said. "I told him that I left the hotel about 12:15 or 12:20 o'clock with the bell captain and that we drove to a restaurant on Patton Avenue and bought sandwiches. From there we went straight home in the bell captain's car."[335]

Denying that he had noticed Helen during her time at the hotel and insisting that he saw nothing unusual the night of the murder, Roddy was locked in a cell for the night.[336]

"Could he have been [at the hotel] at 1 o'clock?" a reporter called after Brown as the Sheriff left his office for the day.

"That's something I'm trying to determine at this time," Brown said, putting on his hat.[337]

By the following morning officers had dismissed the notion that Roddy and Fleming visited Helen's room together while she was a guest. Other information, however, had been made public about Roddy, which caused the sheriff to keep him imprisoned.[338]

Though manager Pat Branch asserted that Roddy was a "trustworthy servant" who had worked for him "off and on one or two years," it soon came out that just two days before his arrest, Roddy had been fired from the hotel after a guest complained that he was "fresh" with her. She said that when she asked to be taken to the mezzanine floor, he instead took her to the roof garden and made improper advances.[339]

When questioned about his dismissal from the hotel by the press, Roddy denied the allegations, instead telling reporters that he quit after he argued with one of the hotel managers about "keeping an elevator at the roof garden of the hotel too long." He explained that he was delayed on the roof when two female hotel guests asked him to move chairs for them so that they could sit in the garden.[340]

Asked for a statement about holding Roddy, Sheriff Brown replied "with a grin: 'I'm holding [him] for a board bill. All colored boys have board bills.'"[341]

After Roddy spent more than a week in jail without being questioned, his family employed Sanford Brown, an Asheville attorney, to "obtain his release, on a habeas corpus writ if necessary."[342]

By the time the attorney arrived at the sheriff's office with the proper documentation and asked Sheriff Brown if he was planning on releasing Roddy, the sheriff replied, "Why he has been out for more than two hours." And in fact, Roddy was already back at home. "He has a wife and two children to feed. I think he's been in jail long enough," Sheriff Brown said.[343]

With Roddy's release, the *Philadelphia Tribune*, a Black-run newspaper, reported, "Puzzled local authorities, who have made a mess of the investigation are now reported to be looking for a white man, 'young, well-educated, soft-voiced, athletic, about six feet tall, weighs 160 to 170 pounds and knows the layout of the hotel.'"[344]


As JULY TURNED INTO August, new leads were dwindling, and only Daniel Gaddy, the night watchman, remained in jail.

"And Gaddy, I believe, is also innocent of the crime itself," Sheriff Brown told his deputies.[345]

Deputies Tom Brown and Love Gudger lamented, "Exhaustive questioning of witness after witness! Over two hundred people whose every movement, every word, [was] tracked down and verified. And we got exactly nowhere....Long arduous hours of routine backtracking, delving into the histories of countless suspects, ceaseless shadowing of hotel employees. And we were as much in the dark as the day when we first stepped into the blood-spattered room of the murdered girl."[346]

"What was the origin of the mysterious twelfth key?" they asked. "Where was the lethal weapon concealed? Had the crime been one of passion, revenge, robbery? What did Gaddy know? Was the killer still in Asheville or had he fled thousands of miles away?"[347]

These unanswered questions taunted the investigators and carried an especially heavy weight for Sheriff Brown, who was simultaneously campaigning for reelection. It seemed like the murder would never be solved.

With no new developments in the case, reporters from out of town began returning home. News stories about Helen's murder, mostly rehashing details that had previously been reported, no longer made the headlines of the daily papers, instead pushed below the fold or further into the pages. As one reporter explained, "The hot murder mystery that brought me and other newspapermen from Eastern cities to Asheville is cold now. If they ever get the man who killed Helen Clevenger in her hotel room it will be because of some lucky break that is not now in sight....Then begins a long, tedious hunt for new clues....It is in the unspectacular part of an investigation that detectives can show their genius. But it doesn't make newspaper copy."[348]

Behind the scenes, unbeknownst to reporters, the investigation was taking a speedy U-turn with the arrival of Walter B. Orr, the former police chief of Charlotte, North Carolina. Described by deputies as "lynx-eyed, soft-spoken, erect as a Uhlan lancer," Orr, at the time, was one of the better-known officers in the state. "An arch-foe of crime and criminals,"[349] Orr was best known as the police chief who, in 1919 during his first year on the job, was tasked with bringing the Charlotte streetcar drivers' strike under control. As strikers and sympathizers began marching, Orr shouted, "Get back every damn one of you." He pulled his gun and began shooting. His fellow officers followed suit. Five on the picket line were killed and fourteen hospitalized. No officers or strikebreakers were injured. Though thirty-one officers were charged in the deaths of the strikers, a judge dismissed the case just two weeks later.[350]

"Listen, fellows," Orr told the Buncombe County deputies in a "soft, Southern drawl," "don't let me butt into this picture too much, but if you want me to tell you what I think, I'll do it."

"Go ahead," the deputies chorused, nodding.

"All right. We've been living with this case too much! Our minds have been muddled with a hundred and one clews [*sic*]—all of them worthless. A real clew might be stuck under our noses and we might let it pass. Let's forget everything. Put the dead stuff out of your minds and go right back to the beginning. Durham Jones, Casey Jones, Pittman—they all saw the killer. Let's go back and question them again and again. Somewhere we'll hit something—and it will mean pay dirt," Orr finished with a flourish.[351]

And so they did. The deputies went back to Helen's room, meticulously combing through items, opening drawers, flipping through the telephone book, inspecting the walls and the ceiling, but to no avail. They spoke with Durham Jones and then Casey Jones, who had both witnessed an unknown man leap the balustrade, even working with them to reenact the escape—much to the delight of passersby. But this too was a dead end.[352]

Finally, the only witness left to reinterview was Erwin Pittman, the bank examiner who lodged in the room across from Helen's that night. Pittman arrived back in Asheville at the beginning of August.[353]

THERE ARE TWO ACCOUNTS of what happened next. In October 1936, a pulp magazine, *Official Detective Stories*, released the account of two of Brown's deputies, Love Gudger and Tom Brown. This version began with Orr calling Pittman back to Asheville.

INSIDE STORY of the CAMDEN DOBBINS MURDER
SEX BEHIND BARS — More Sensational Revelations
THE RAPIST KILLING of CO-ED CLEVENGER

Cover of the October 1936 issue of *Official Detective Stories. Author's collection.*

"Tell us again, Mr. Pittman, every movement, every word you spoke, from the time you heard the scream until you had closed your door on the shadow-figure," Orr requested.

Pittman's story remained the same. He talked for over half an hour, telling of hearing a scream, going out to investigate and finding an empty hallway and then seeing a shadowy figure in the doorway to room 224 and the words they exchanged.

Brown stopped him. "Were those the exact words of the mysterious shadow: 'That's what I'm wondering, too?'"

Pittman leaned forward. "I've been thinking about that," he said slowly, considering his response.

"He either said, 'that's what I'm wondering, too' or 'it's what I'm wondering, too.' Anyway, one word doesn't make a lot of difference," Pittman said with an anxious laugh.

The gray-haired Orr immediately looked to the sheriff and then quickly back at Pittman and said softly, "A whale of a difference son—I believe!"

Understanding Orr's implications, Sheriff Brown stood, towering over the seated Pittman. "Then, Mr. Pittman, you are undecided as to which remark the man made, but you are inclined to believe he said: 'it's what I'm wondering, too!' Is that correct?"

"That's right," Pittman said, nodding in agreement.

"Boys, we're on our way," the sheriff declared, unable to hide his excitement. "We can eliminate nearly eighty suspects. That leaves us twenty-six."

With the narrowing of the suspect field by nearly three-quarters, the deputies finally understood what Orr and Brown thought they had deduced from Pittman's statement.

"*The killer's identity revolved around one little word—'it's'? That was the remark of a Negro—not a white man!* [emphasis theirs] That was one of the peculiarities of the Southern Negro's speech, the use of 'it' where a white would ordinarily use 'that,'" explained the deputies for magazine readers who might not have grasped the syntactical nuance.[354] This "break" in the case and shift in the investigation was not immediately released to the press.[355]

In an alternate version of events, released just before election day and co-authored by Sheriff Brown, Brown noted that Pittman returned to Asheville of his own volition and "dropped in" to see the sheriff.

"You know, Sheriff," Pittman said, "I've been thinking over the words of the fellow who stood in the doorway of 224 that night, and I have about reached the conclusion that I did not quote him correctly, or rather, that I did not quote him exactly."

Pittman leaned toward the sheriff. "I told you the man said: 'That is what I was wondering myself,' and I really believe now that what he said was: 'It's what I'se wonderin', too'!"

Hearing these words, "the picture of a man came to [Brown's] mind—the picture of a Negro. The kind of man who would whisper: 'It's what I'se wonderin', too!'"

Excited, Sheriff Brown thanked Pittman for this new information, and as soon as Pittman left, the sheriff called in his deputies.

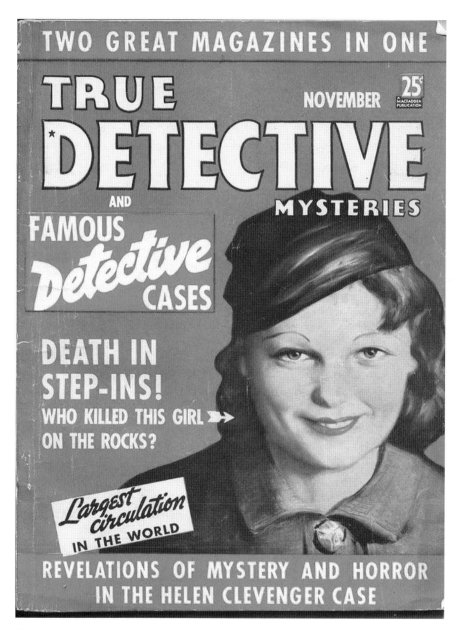

Cover of the November 1936 issue of *True Detective Mysteries*. *Author's collection.*

A man stands in the doorway to room 220 and points at room 224 to illustrate the view Erwin Pittman had of the unknown figure in Helen's doorway. *E.M. Ball Photographic Collection, D.H. Ramsey Library Special Collections, UNC–Asheville, 28804.*

"I believe we've been barking up the wrong tree. We've been busy eliminating white men who could have committed this crime. Now, we're going to work on the Negroes."[356]

Regardless of how it happened behind closed doors, with this new "evidence" in hand, the investigators effectively eliminated all white men from the suspect pool. They focused on the Battery Park's Black male employees under the assumption that the person who committed the crime was familiar with the layout of the hotel. Since the only people of color allowed inside the hotel for any length of time were employees, it seemed most likely to them that only a current employee would have been able to gain access to the hotel that night and quickly escape. Investigators made no mention, however, of why an employee would attempt an escape out the front entrance of the hotel rather than the rear employee entrance.[357]

BACK IN HIS OFFICE, the sheriff reached into his desk drawer and pulled out a battered file folder. He produced a single sheet of paper.

"Here's a list of the twenty-six Negro employees at the Battery Park. We'll divide 'em up. The majority already have been questioned two and three times, and might give us the debutante yawn. But pound at 'em. The man who went to the girl's room that night knew his way around—and he's got a gun that will fit the exploded shell we've recovered. Pittman's shadow may be among those twenty-six! If he's not—well, go ahead now!" the Sheriff shouted at his men.[358]

For the next five days, the deputies brought in each Black employee "who had not been definitely eliminated"[359] and subjected them to "ceaseless questioning, interrogating, grilling,"[360] eventually narrowing down twenty-six to five, three because they were known to own guns.[361]

After comparing the three pistols with the shell from the murder scene and finding no match, the five were whittled down to two—Banks Taylor, a "pantry boy," and L.D. Roddy, who had previously been held and released.[362] When neither revealed any new information, they were "locked up…[to] improve their memories."[363]

For the next few days, the sheriff refused to speak with reporters, who had no knowledge of Taylor and Roddy's detention. Local newspaper coverage waned. The morning edition of the August 9 issue of the *Asheville Citizen* included only a short article five pages deep acknowledging Gaddy's fourth week in prison.[364] But just a few hours later, with the release of an extra edition of the paper, Helen's murder investigation was back in the headlines.

## 7

# HE GOT A .32 AUTOMATIC.
# WHY DON'T YOU WORRY HIM?

T he public was anxious. The unsolved murder was giving Asheville "a black eye," which was "affecting the tourist trade, and was seriously damaging the section." And as the November election drew nearer, Sheriff Brown was getting desperate.[365]

He began writing letters. He wrote to a tour company that had lodged guests at the hotel that night, asking for the names and addresses of everyone in the group; he wrote to the chief of police in Winchester, Virginia, asking for a "confidential investigation" into the character and whereabouts of one of the town's residents; and he wrote to the chief of the homicide squad in New York City asking to interview Helen's friends and family to find out if she owned a pistol.[366]

Just over a week after the sheriff posted his letters, two "crack detectives," Sergeant Thomas Martin and Detective John J. Quinn from the New York Police Department, walked into Brown's office, offering to help with the investigation. Thomas Martin, stout and balding, wore circular horn-rimmed glasses. He was a seasoned detective and had just come off of solving the sensational rape and murder of Nancy Titterton, a New York writer and the wife of an NBC executive. The press had already been making comparisons between the two murder cases, primary because both Nancy and Helen were young, attractive white women. Martin solved the Titterton murder by tracing the distinctive cord used to tie Nancy's hands to the upholstery shop where the Tittertons had sent a couch for repair; the solve made him a minor celebrity.[367]

July 30th, 1936.

Chief of Homicide Squad,
Centre Street Headquarters,
Metropolitan Police Department,
New York City.

Dear Sir;- In re: Helen Clevenger.

I will appreciate very much if you will have someone interview Mr. and Mrs. J. F. Clevenger at 93 Howton
Street, Great Kills, Staten Island, the parents of the
above named who was murdered in a hotel in this city. I
would like to know if Helen owned a pistol of any kind
and if it is possible that she could have had one with
her here. Mr. Clevenger's business address is, U. S.
Department of Agriculture, Food and Drug Administration, New York City. Also please interview Helen's
friends and school mates at the New York University
and if there is any angle to Mr. Clevenger's work or
duties that might make vindictive enemies. I will
appreciate very much if you will have these angles
investigated and communicate with me as soon as possible.

Thanking you for this, I am

Very truly yours,

Laurence E. Brown,
Sheriff, Buncombe Co.

LEB/m

Letter from Sheriff Laurence Brown to chief of the homicide squad, New York City Police Department, July 30, 1936. *Laurence Brown Collection, Swannanoa Valley Museum & History Center, Black Mountain, North Carolina.*

Stocky and wavy-haired Quinn, a relatively new detective, followed Martin's lead. The pair of white men spent the next two days with the Asheville investigators going over every detail.

With all the evidence on the table, Sergeant Martin asked the sheriff, "What is your best lead?"

"My best lead is in jail," Brown replied, referring to Banks Taylor. "I think we better work on it."[368]

So they went to the jail and "began hammering anew"[369] at the twenty-two-year-old. After a "grilling" by officers, Taylor admitted that he owned a gun but told them he had given the gun to his father several weeks prior.

The deputies escorted Taylor to his father's house, where they recovered the weapon from a trunk in the home. Though it was the right kind of pistol—a .32 automatic—"considerably to [their] disappointment," the deputies found that the gun contained eight unexploded shells and "appeared not to have been fired in a long time." The shells did not bear any similarity to the one found in Helen's room.[370] They still had not found the murder weapon.

The deputies stopped to relay this information to the sheriff.

"Taylor lied once and finally told us about this. He may be holding back something else," Sergeant Martin suggested. "Let's question him again."

They escorted Taylor back to the jail, where they began questioning him in relays—still with no result. But just before midnight, tiring, Taylor complained to the officers, "What you worryin' me so much for? Martin Moore got a gun. He got a .32 automatic. Why don't you worry him?"

"How do you know Moore has a .32 automatic?" Sheriff Brown queried the young man.

"Cause when that murder happened I told Martin Moore: 'Do you know that girl was shot with an automatic just like yours? I sure am glad I gave mine to my old man.' And then Martin said: 'Yeah, it don't worry me none 'cause I lent mine to Lem Roddy two days before the girl got killed.'" Taylor replied.

"Do you know whether Moore really lent his gun to Roddy?" asked Brown.

"Naw, he didn't tell me any more than that," Taylor said, "but I think he's lying."

"What makes you think Moore is lying?" pressed Sheriff Brown.

"Cause I asked Roddy before you arrested him and he said he didn't get any gun from Martin," Taylor replied. "I'd rather believe Lem Roddy."[371]

Martin Moore, a twenty-two-year-old hallboy at the hotel, had been briefly questioned and released along with the larger group of Black hotel employees days before. The sheriff remembered him as a "big black fellow, who stood a head taller than the others…[with] a powerful pair of shoulders and arms that came almost to his knees."[372]

Still suspicious of Taylor and Roddy but willing to follow any lead, the sheriff turned to his deputies and said, "Let's go after Moore."[373]

Martin Moore's home at 84½ Hill Street in Asheville, 1936. *E.M. Ball Photographic Collection, D.H. Ramsey Library Special Collections, UNC–Asheville, 28804.*

Moore lived with his mother at 84½ Hill Street—the same street where Banks Taylor and Lem Roddy lived—in a small wooden house not far from the hotel.

It was past midnight when Deputies Tom Brown and Love Gudger, along with Sergeant Martin and Detective Quinn, arrived at the house and pounded on the door. Martin's mother, Celie, answered.

The deputies would later relate to a magazine writer their version of what happened when they entered the Moore home, pushed passed Celie without a word and stepped through the small kitchen into the single bedroom, lit only by the beams of their flashlights.

Searching the room, their lights fell on a sleeping face. Startled at the sudden disturbance, Martin Moore sat up quickly. He slid his feet to the floor, blinking as his eyes adjusted to the lights pointed in his direction.

Sergeant Martin took the lead, "Give me that gun you killed that girl with!"

"I ain't got no gun," Moore said, fully awake now.

"Come on, boy, tell them the truth," Banks Taylor interjected. "Tell them where the gun is. I done saw you with it."

"All right," Moore conceded. "I own a gun, but I lent it to Roddy."

"Has Roddy got it now?" one of the investigators asked.

"No, sir, he gave it back a day after that girl got killed." Moore told them.

"Well, where is it?" demanded Sergeant Martin.

"Wait til I dress and I'll take you to it. It's outside," Moore said, standing up to pull on his clothes. Officers handcuffed each of Moore's wrists to one of their own, and they walked out to the back of the house.[374]

Back in the yard, Moore pointed at the wooden steps. "It's right there under the porch on a rafter," he told them. Deputy Tom Brown, flashlight in hand, got down on hands and knees and shimmied under the porch. As he told it, his light swept over the support beams and there on a foundation rafter was a "snub-nosed automatic." Tom, nervous that a string or piano wire could be attached to the trigger as a booby-trap, took his time retrieving the gun. As he emerged from under the house, the other officers trained their lights on his hand. There they saw what they had been looking for, a .32 automatic pistol covered with "several bloodstains and two blonde little hairs, like fuzz from a human face."[375]

"You killed that girl!" shouted Detective Quinn.[376]

"Honest, boss, I didn't kill her," Moore told him. "That's my gun, but I done loaned it to L.D. He done took the gun several days before the trouble happened up at the hotel."[377]

"You come with us," Deputy Brown ordered as he shoved Moore into the back of the department car. "We'll have a talk with Roddy and see what he says."[378]

The deputies took Moore straight to the courthouse for questioning.[379] The group of white men hit Martin with a barrage of questions. Moore stuck to his story. He had lent the gun to Roddy two days before the murder and got it back the day after the murder while he visited Roddy at his grandmother's house on Hill Street.[380]

An unnamed and "badly frightened" witness confirmed Moore's story. "Yes. Martin told me he let L.D. have his gun. Said he was scared L.D. done got himself in trouble."[381]

By 1:30 a.m., the officers went back to Hill Street and picked up Roddy—who had been released the day before—for a third time.[382]

Sheriff Laurence Brown stands at his desk and examines the pistol allegedly found under Martin Moore's home, August 1936. *E.M. Ball Photographic Collection, D.H. Ramsey Library Special Collections, UNC–Asheville, 28804.*

RODDY "WITHSTOOD A SEVERE grilling,"[383] denying that he had borrowed Moore's pistol. "That big ape's trying to frame me," Deputy Brown remembered Roddy saying.[384]

While several deputies continued to question Roddy, others began examining the weapon more closely. "The butt was encrusted with a dark, gummy substance that appeared to be blood. The magazine held several cartridges. They bore the same 'H' and three stars as the empty shell found in Miss Clevenger's bathroom."[385]

Now convinced they had finally found the murder weapon but with conflicting information about who was in possession of the weapon on the night of the murder, one of the officers suggested, "Let's put them together to talk it over."[386]

The officers handcuffed Banks Taylor and Martin Moore together and placed them in a small room. Roddy, also handcuffed, was brought in soon afterward. Unbeknownst to the handcuffed men, the officers had recently installed a small Dictaphone nearby.[387]

Walter Orr quietly took a seat in the adjoining room, observing the men through an open door. Down the hall, Sheriff Brown, Detective Quinn, Sergeant Martin and Deputies Brown and Gudger put on headphones.[388]

Over the wire, the officers reported hearing Banks Taylor speak first: "Don't be a damn fool. Go ahead and tell them. I know you ain't loaned that gun to Roddy."

"Don't tell me what to do, big boy. I lent that gun to Roddy. I say, I ought to know what I done," Martin Moore replied quickly.

"You're a damn liar!" Lem Roddy shot back. "You ain't ever done no such thing."

"I know he is," Taylor said to Roddy. "He can't get away with it. Them Sheriffs are going to get him into more trouble than he is now."

"Mind your own business!" Moore told Taylor.[389]

According to the deputies, the "heated accusation and counter-accusation" continued until the men "nearly came to blows" and were quickly separated by Orr, who "rushed in from the courtroom next door.[390]

Orr shut the door on his way out. Taylor and Roddy continued to hammer at Moore, telling him to confess and "take them off the spot."[391] But Moore would admit to nothing and sat in sullen silence for several minutes, ignoring Taylor and Roddy.[392]

Growing impatient, Sergeant Martin yanked off his headphones. Standing up, he said, "I think he'll say something now if we go back there. This may keep up until daybreak. Let's look at them again."[393]

The investigators joined the trio in the small room.

"Listen," Sergeant Martin said. "The zero hour is here. If you get what I mean. Either one or all three of you will pay for the murder of that girl. Which will it be?"[394]

At that moment—just before 4:30 a.m.—Detective Martin burst in the room, a white fingerprint card in hand, and made a carefully rehearsed accusation.[395]

"It's all right, Sheriff," Detective Martin shouted. "This man's fingerprints were found on the gun and on that lampshade in Miss Clevenger's room. He killed her."[396] In reality, neither the gun nor the lampshade had any usable fingerprints on them.[397]

"There was two fingerprints on that gun, and one of them was Roddy's," Moore replied.

"You're wrong," interjected Orr. "Roddy's fingerprints weren't on the gun. Just yours."

Martin Moore, 1936. *North Carolina Collection, Pack Memorial Public Library, Asheville, North Carolina.*

Leaning back against the wall, Quinn continued, "Yes, sir, big fellow, those fingerprints kind of gave you away. They always do. Why don't you talk and save yourself a lot of trouble?"[398]

Sheriff Brown gently said to Moore, "Want to get this thing off your mind by telling us all about it?"

Then, according to the investigators, Moore shook his "gorillalike" shoulders and mumbled,[399] "Yes, I killed her."

"Tell us about it," the sheriff replied. "Then you'll feel better. This thing has been troubling you a lot, hasn't it?"[400]

"All right, I'll tell you all about it! I shot the girl 'cause I had to! She screamed too much. There wasn't nothing else for me to do but pull the trigger!"[401]

# I AIN'T NEVER KNOWN HIM TO MISS.

Born on May 15, 1914, Martin Moore grew up just outside Pauline, South Carolina, in Glenn Springs Township, about seventy-five miles southeast of Asheville. His parents, Celie and John Moore, had lived in Pauline since before the turn of the twentieth century—and in South Carolina since they were born in the early 1870s. They were part of the first generation of Black children in the state who were not born into slavery.

Not far from Glenn Springs stands Walnut Grove Plantation, once home to Charles and Mary Moore, who began enslaving people in Moore, South Carolina, prior to the American Revolution. Besides Charles and Mary, at least a dozen other white men and women with the last name "Moore" held people captive in and around Spartanburg County on various plantations.[402] After emancipation, it would not have been unusual for newly free people to take the surname of their former enslavers. It is possible, perhaps likely, that Martin Moore's paternal grandparents were enslaved near where he would be born fifty years later. Certainly, his maternal grandmother, Annie Watts, a widow in 1900 who lived with her son's family, spent the first half of her life enslaved in the state.[403]

As early as 1900, the family rented a farm on the Appalachian Highway in Pauline, likely working the land as sharecroppers. Martin's siblings, as young as eight years old, labored daily on the farm. By the time of Martin's birth, his forty-year-old mother, who had married when she was just fifteen years old, had birthed twelve other children and already buried three. It is likely that her husband, John, died soon after, or even before, Martin's birth. Martin was the youngest in the family.[404]

After John's death, Celie's oldest son, Napoleon, and his wife took over the family's farm share. Celie, who had never had the opportunity to attend school, began washing clothes to make ends meet while her older children farmed. And though her children were not able to attend school for long, she made sure they all learned to read and write.[405]

Sometime before 1925, Napoleon's wife likely passed away, and he remarried a young woman from North Carolina. The couple soon relocated to Richmond, Virginia, where Napoleon would find factory work and the couple would raise their children.[406] Though Celie still had family in Glenn Springs, it is likely that around the same time Napoleon decided to leave sharecropping behind, Celie moved with her two youngest children to Asheville.[407] The reason for their move north remains unclear, but Martin later confirmed that the family "first was here [in Asheville] in 1923 and stayed a year and came back about 1925."[408]

But certainly, by the time the census taker came through on April 10, 1930, Celie, now almost fifty years old; her eighteen-year-old daughter, Alice; and fifteen-year-old Martin had moved into a small house on Gudger Street in Asheville. Celie continued taking in laundry to pay the fifteen dollars a month due to her landlord, and Alice, who worked as a servant for a private family, brought in money as well. The family supplemented their income by hosting a boarder in their small home.[409]

Martin attended the nearby segregated Hill Street School through the sixth grade, dropping out to do odd jobs and help support his family. Soon he and his mother moved to a home at 84½ Hill Street, and Martin took a job at the Battery Park Hotel, just three blocks away.[410]

By the summer of 1936, Martin had worked at the hotel for nearly three years as a full-time hallman. He made twelve dollars a week and was considered an exemplary employee.[411] But in the early hours of August 9, 1936, surrounded by six white officers—including Sheriff Laurence Brown and the two detectives from New York City—Martin signed a confession after hours of questioning without a lawyer present. It read, in part:

> *When I sneaked back into the hotel through back door I had the same thirty-two automatic pistol that you have, down front of my trousers, at 12:45 A.M., July 16ᵗʰ, and went to second floor to sneak in some rooms to look for money. I tried doors on rooms 218 and 219. They would not open. Next room I tried was room 224. I believed the young girl was in there....*

Martin Moore, 1936. *E.M. Ball Photographic Collection, D.H. Ramsey Library Special Collections, UNC–Asheville, 28804.*

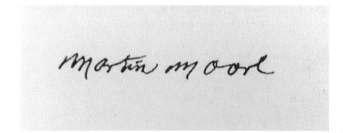

Martin Moore's signature on his statement, made in room 509, County Courthouse, Asheville, August 9, 1936. *D.H. Ramsey Library, Special Collections, UNC–Asheville.*

*I did not steal anything from this girl's room. I got scared. I figured she was not in the room. My reason was that I found the door unlocked, but when I got in she was there and she screamed. That's why I shot her....*

*When I entered room she said, "What do you want." I told her I opened door, I did not know she was in there. I looked at her and she said, "I am going to scream." I told her not to. So she screamed once. I closed the door. She said, "You'd better get out of here or I'll call the office." I was standing close to her and I shot her before she could go back and I hit her with the butt. She fell on her knees, she screamed again and I hit her again, she screamed again and I hit her twice....I unscrewed shade and bulb from socket and placed it some where and came out. As I was about to leave room some man standing in the doorway said, "what was the screams", and I said to man, "It's what I was wondering." I then closed door, went down front steps to mezzanine floor and down mezzanine to ball room.*

*From ball room I passed through a heavy door and screen door, reached porch, climbed on bannister, slid down half way and jumped and then ran to my right on a street west of the hotel to Montford Street and started walking on Hill Street....I had on a rain coat, a black sleeveless sweater, don't know what shirt or trousers. I wore a brown cap. The brown cap you showed me, I wore.*

*I make this statement of my own free will and accord, and without promise or threat of any kind whatsoever.*[412]

With the signed confession in hand, Sheriff Brown called reporters to his office to give them the "essential points necessary to write their story" on the condition that they would not release the information until 12:30 p.m. Brown needed time for Martin to reenact the crime. And the reenactment needed to firmly fit with eyewitness accounts of the murderer's escape.

But even without a news release, word quickly spread that another arrest had been made in the Clevenger case. Crowds began to gather behind the courthouse and around the hotel to determine if the rumors were true.

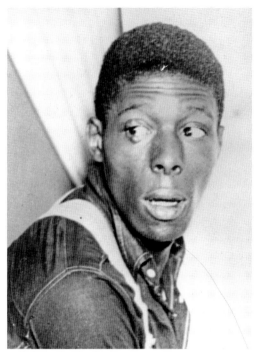

*Left*: Martin Moore, August 9, 1936. *ACME Newspictures, author's collection.*

*Below*: Deputy Love Gudger (*left*) handcuffed to Martin Moore at the back entrance to the Battery Park Hotel during the reenactment, August 9, 1936. *E.M. Ball Photographic Collection, D.H. Ramsey Library Special Collections, UNC–Asheville, 28804.*

They were not disappointed. Soon after Brown spoke to reporters, a large group, including an official court stenographer and photographer, but still no lawyer, escorted Moore from the courthouse to the Battery Park Hotel.

Martin entered the alleyway behind the hotel handcuffed to Deputy Love Gudger. He wore suspenders that hitched his pants up above his waist and made his arms seem impossibly long. The news media would soon write long physical descriptions of the lanky young man, published alongside the text of his confession. "His face is angular, for a negro, the jaws being rather flat. His right eyelids are thick, giving his face a rather sinister appearance, as if he were squinting," wrote a *Citizen* reporter. "Moore's hands are huge and his shoulders are powerful. While he appears angular and even bony, there is a suggestion of great strength in his figure. He moves in a quick cat-like way."[413]

The sheriff instructed Moore to show them every step he took on the night of Helen's murder. The large group entered through the hotel's rear entrance and navigated down the long, tiled aisle leading to the employees' quarters in the hotel's basement.

"Did you see anybody on this floor?"

"No sir," Moore replied.

Sheriff Brown asked Moore to clarify. "You went straight from the back door right on through to the stairsteps?"

"Yes sir. I went right here to this locker room. I went in and hid. I went in here where I could hide."

The group stepped into the employee locker room and gathered around Moore.

"What did you do all that time from about 9 o'clock until around 12:45?" one of the men asked Moore.

"I read a book."

"Then you went back this way?" one of the investigators asked, pointing out the door and into the hallway.

"Yes," Moore said, leading the pack of officials down the hallway and up the staircase to the second floor.

"Show us the first door that you tried to open."

Moore stepped over to room 218 and pretended to turn the door knob. "It was locked."[414]

Night watchman Daniel Gaddy, however, had already told officers that during his one o'clock round of the hotel he may have forgotten to punch the time clock because "I saw the door to room 218 open and that worried me." Since the occupant was asleep when Gaddy poked his head in the room, he left the door open.[415]

"What door did you go to next?"

"Next I went to 219."[416] This room was just to the left of 218.[417]

"Was that door locked?"

"Yes, sir."

"Where did you go when you left that door?"

"224,"[418] Moore replied. The group turned and headed farther down the hall, away from the stairwell and the elevators. They passed the doorway to room 220 on their right without stopping. It was here that E.B. Pittman had stood and witnessed a man in Helen's doorway shortly after her murder.[419] Martin stopped at the door to room 224.

"When you came to this door it was locked?" one of the men asked.

"No, sir."

Deputy Sheriff Tom Brown made his way to the front of the group and unlocked the door. He pushed it open.

"When you came to this door and opened it how far did you go inside before you saw the girl?"

In answer, Moore walked past the officials and stopped just past the bathroom door, about four feet in front of the threshold but still in the room's entryway.

"What did you say?"

"I said I didn't know she was in here. Then she said, 'I am going to call the office and going to scream,'" Moore continued. "I told her not to."

"Did she scream?"

"She screamed once and walked up close to me. Then I backed like this, about that far back. Then she screamed again. Then I shot her." Moore said.

"Indicate where you think you shot her," one of the men instructed Moore.

"About there." Moore said, indicating a spot on one of the officer's chests.

"Is that the right place or was it higher?"

"It was about there." Moore said again, pointing an unloaded gun at the left side of the man's sternum, around the fourth rib.

Not completely satisfied that Moore had indicated the correct location of the bullet wound, one of the men asked Moore to then point out on a shorter man, Deputy Love Gudger, where he shot Helen Clevenger. Moore complied.

"You had the muzzle pointing down with your finger on the trigger?"

"Yes."

"When did you take the shade off here?" one of the men asked, as he indicated the light fixture attached to the headboard.

"I saw her fall on her knees. When I hit her right here, I walked over by the bed." Moore said as he walked the few steps from the entryway to the single bed.

"Show how you took the light off."

"Take this," Moore handed the gun to one of the men.

"Did you use both hands to take it off?"

"One."

"Show us how you did that."

Moore proceeded to unscrew the bulb from its fixture with some difficulty, as his right hand had now been cuffed to Deputy Gudger's. Gudger climbed onto the bed to allow Moore to access the bulb.

"When you took this shade off the light where did you lay it?"

"I don't remember."

"Do you think that you laid it on this chair?"

"I dropped it. I think I dropped it."

"Take it off and put it on this chair. If you think you put it on the chair," one of the men instructed Moore. "Take it off all the way. Lay it down the same way as you laid it down before."

"Yes," Moore said, holding the bulb and shade.

"Lay it down where you think that you put it."

"Here." With difficulty, Moore placed the bulb and small lampshade on the green upholstered bedside chair, pulling Deputy Gudger, the pair still cuffed together, across the bed.

Now that Moore had finally placed the shade and bulb in the same position that the murderer had placed them weeks prior, the officials moved on.

"Show how you hit her after you came from the bed," the sheriff instructed. Deputy Gudger, uncuffing himself from Martin, got on his knees, facing the door. Behind Gudger, the stenographer hurriedly jotted notes on a white pad. The photographer began taking a series of images, the flashbulb exploding every few minutes.

"I hit her here," Moore said, placing the gun against Gudger's left cheek.

"Did she scream then?"

"Yes and then she went back like this and tried to get up after I hit her. Then I hit her only once on the floor. I hit her twice after she was on the floor."

"Show the position she was in when she laid down like that."

Deputy Gudger laid on the floor on his back, his feet almost crossing the threshold into the hallway. Moore bent at the waist and placed the butt of the gun against Gudger's cheek yet again as Sheriff Brown leaned over to get a better view.

Martin Moore places a lightbulb on the chair while handcuffed to Deputy Love Gudger. Sheriff Laurence Brown watches, August 9, 1936. *E.M. Ball Photographic Collection, D.H. Ramsey Library Special Collections, UNC–Asheville, 28804.*

Martin Moore is instructed to point a gun at Deputy Love Gudger inside room 224 at the Battery Park Hotel, August 9, 1936. *E.M. Ball Photographic Collection, D.H. Ramsey Library Special Collections, UNC–Asheville, 28804.*

*Above*: Deputy Love Gudger kneels on the floor of room 224 while Martin Moore places the pistol against his cheek as instructed, August 9, 1936. *E.M. Ball Photographic Collection, D.H. Ramsey Library Special Collections, UNC–Asheville, 28804.*

*Opposite, top*: Martin Moore demonstrates how the murderer hit Helen Clevenger, represented by Deputy Love Gudger, with the butt of the pistol. Sheriff Laurence Brown (*left*) and other officials watch, August 9, 1936. *E.M. Ball Photographic Collection, D.H. Ramsey Library Special Collections, UNC–Asheville, 28804.*

*Opposite, bottom*: Martin Moore stands in the doorway to room 224, illustrating where the man in the doorway stood the night of the murder, August 9, 1936. *E.M. Ball Photographic Collection, D.H. Ramsey Library Special Collections, UNC–Asheville, 28804.*

"What did you do after you hit her that time?"

"I opened the bathroom door and my feet struck her. I had to pull the door back," Moore said, closing the bathroom door. "Then I went around like this and shut the outside door."

"Because her body was lying here you had to pull this door back?"

"Yes. When I got to the door I saw a man was standing in that door," Moore said, pointing at the door diagonally across the hall, room 220, which had belonged to Erwin Pittman. "He said, 'What was the screams?' and I said, 'That is what I would like to know.'"

*Above*: Martin Moore, still handcuffed to Deputy Love Gudger, opens the ballroom door to the veranda, August 9, 1936. *E.M. Ball Photographic Collection, D.H. Ramsey Library Special Collections, UNC–Asheville, 28804.*

*Opposite, top*: Martin Moore exits from the ballroom to the veranda, handcuffed to Deputy Love Gudger, August 9, 1936. *E.M. Ball Photographic Collection, D.H. Ramsey Library Special Collections, UNC–Asheville, 28804.*

*Opposite, bottom*: Martin Moore hangs off the corner of the Battery Park Hotel's veranda balcony, August 9, 1936. *E.M. Ball Photographic Collection, D.H. Ramsey Library Special Collections, UNC Asheville, 28804.*

"Now be sure to get that right. What did the man over there say. Did he say he was wondering what that fuss was up the hall?" the sheriff pressed Moore.

"I said, 'It is what I was wondering,'" Moore replied. Out in the hallway, the photographer captured an image of Moore looking out of the room toward room 220.

"When you were standing there, how long before the man in 220 opened the door?"

"I don't know. Just as I opened the door. Then he said 'I wonder what the screams was.' I said, 'That is what I was wondering too.'" Martin again forgot to say *it* instead of *that*. This time the sheriff ignored the mistake.

Officials watch as Martin Moore tries to climb down the side of the hotel to the street level, August 9, 1936. *E.M. Ball Photographic Collection, D.H. Ramsey Library Special Collections, UNC–Asheville, 28804.*

"Did you answer him the first time he spoke?"

"Yes. Then he closed the door and went back in his room. Then I came out and closed her door."

The group crowded back into the hallway and Deputy Gudger again handcuffed himself to Martin.

"Which way did you go?"

Moore turned right down the hallway toward the stairwell and the elevator. He opened the stairwell door and began descending. "This is the front steps," he told the group.

"You then came on the first floor?"

"Yes," Moore replied as he opened the door and led the way from the front steps to the first-floor hallway and through to the mezzanine to another closed door.

"Did you peep through this door to see if there was anybody on this floor?"

Cab driver Casey Jones points to the location where he saw the unidentified man jump the banister the night of Helen's murder. *E.M. Ball Photographic Collection, D.H. Ramsey Library Special Collections, UNC–Asheville, 28804.*

"Sure, sure," Moore said as the group continued to follow him through the hotel.

"Show how you went."

"This way." Moore led the group into the lobby.

"Did you see anybody in the lobby that night?"

"No, I did not. I stayed close to the wall, down the steps to the ballroom, then into the ballroom. This is just the way I went."[420]

At no point during the reenactment did Moore venture into the manager's office or onto the front porch as eyewitnesses Durham Jones and Casey Jones had seen the intruder do that evening. During the reenactment, Martin chose another path, which took him through the ballroom to the veranda, a half-story above the porch.[421]

"I went right down the outside here," Martin continued, leading the group toward the parapet at the corner of the veranda, leaning slightly over the banister and pointing to street level. As the group peered over the edge, contemplating the more than fifteen-foot drop, they looked out into a crowd of gathering spectators.[422]

Producing the handcuff key, Gudger uncuffed Moore again and, while the photographer got in position, the sheriff told Moore to demonstrate how he made the drop over the banister and down the side of the hotel onto the ground. "I slid about on here. I put my feet here and my hand here and tried to catch here and then I dropped on down....I went down on the sidewalk and I ran from there."[423]

It was a difficult descent, which Martin could only make by slowly lowering himself over the edge, blindly searching for a grip with his toes on a lip in the façade and then jumping down another six feet to the ground. It was also a completely different jump than the one made by the man fleeing the hotel on July 16—a difference of about eight feet in height and half the length of the hotel. It was also inaccessible from the manager's office.

Sheriff Brown explained away this discrepancy by simply stating that Moore lied. "For some reason he doesn't want to say he went to the hotel manager's office," Sheriff Brown asserted.[424]

With the reenactment concluded, one of the men asked Moore, "You said you knew the Sheriff would get you?"

"Yes."

"How did you know?"

"I told you."

"What did you tell me?" the man pressed, playing to the reporters now surrounding them.

"I ain't never known him to miss."[425]

## 9

# MAYBE IT WAS ALL BEING HUSHED UP.

With a more-or-less successful reenactment, Sheriff Brown was ready to let the world know that the murderer had been apprehended. His midday embargo on the story passed, and moments later, the *Asheville Citizen-Times* released an extra edition of the paper, the headline "Negro Arrested for Clevenger Murder, Confesses to Slaying" printed in large, bold type across the page. Under the headline was a photograph of Martin Moore flanked on both sides by all seven arresting officers. They all stare straight into the camera except Sherriff Brown, who looks squarely at Martin Moore.[426]

More than a year later, one of the same *Asheville Citizen* journalists who broke the news of Moore's arrest wrote another article about what he witnessed that day. This article was buried deep in a Sunday edition of the paper. He wrote, "[We] saw the murder reenacted from beginning to end. Curious crowds who watched the reenactment knew what was going on, but weren't quite sure the negro had done the killing."[427]

In August 1936, however, the *Citizen* told the sheriff's story. And people were eager to read it. Hundreds of people gathered outside Asheville's newspaper office, wanting to be the first to learn if the rumors that the criminal had been captured were true. Moments later, newspaper boys barely had time to begin yelling, "Extra! Extra!" before they were bombarded by eager purchasers. Cars stopped in the middle of the road so that drivers could grab a paper, with some people buying as many as fifteen copies. That day the *Asheville Citizen-Times* sold more than twenty-five thousand copies of its extra

Officials pose with Martin Moore for the front page of the August 9, 1936 extra edition of the *Asheville Citizen-Times*. (*From left to right*): Buncombe County deputy sheriff Frank Messer, former Charlotte chief of police Walter B. Orr, Buncombe County sheriff Laurence E. Brown, Buncombe County deputy sheriff Love Gudger, Martin Moore, New York City police detective John J. Quinn, Buncombe County deputy sheriff Tom K. Brown and New York City police detective Thomas J. Martin. *Laurence Brown Collection, Swannanoa Valley Museum & History Center, Black Mountain, North Carolina.*

edition—a record for the city, more than double the sales of the previous extra that reported the discovery of the body of Charles A. Lindbergh Jr. in 1932. The presses could not print the papers quickly enough to keep up with demand. Bound stacks of the extra were loaded into cars and rushed to towns around western North Carolina—many of the same towns Helen Clevenger had visited during the final week of her young life.[428]

Helen's mother, still convalescing in New York, was "elated" when she learned of the confession. "Isn't that great! We can't save our girl, but other girls can be saved." Still, she added, "I know that sort of thing can't be solved in a day, but it seemed to me for a while that maybe it was all being hushed up."[429]

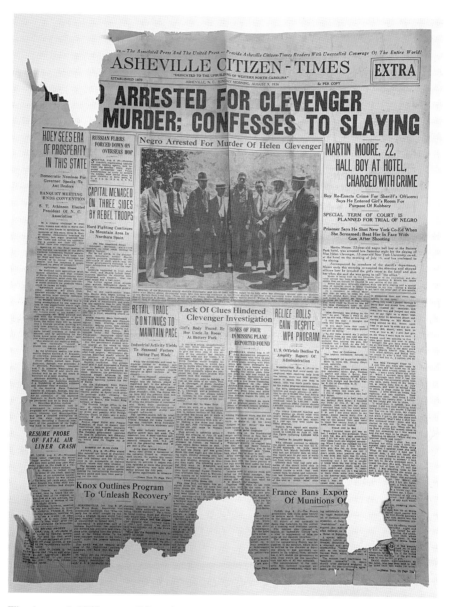

The August 9, 1936 extra edition of the *Asheville Citizen-Times* kept by Sheriff Brown. *Laurence Brown Collection, Swannanoa Valley Museum & History Center, Black Mountain, North Carolina.*

While Helen's family and the white-run *Asheville Citizen* and *Asheville Times* lauded the sheriff for finally apprehending the killer, many Black-run papers in particular were skeptical. The headline in the *Atlanta Daily World* read, "Arrest of 'Slayer'" with *Slayer* in quotation marks.[430] The paper, while expressing a hope that Moore would receive a fair trial and "the truth be established by proved evidence," also lamented, "It is almost unpardonable that a contemporary newspaper gave Jesse Owens not one headline during all of his victories in the Olympics, yet Moore's alleged confession made a front page streamer. This is an old southern custom, obscuring our virtues by screaming from the housetops our sins. Whether Moore is convicted or not, this publicity won't help us."[431]

A week later, in the *Philadelphia Tribune*, another Black-run daily, one unnamed journalist wrote, "For some reason or other—perhaps for no reason at all—that alleged confession made by the bellboy down in Asheville, North Carolina…does not ring true. I just don't believe it. There are ways to make people confess to things they never did. The pistol found was in the wrong place. Why would it be thrown under the front porch? The officials had to pin it on somebody. The girl's parents were complaining bitterly because the murderer had not been caught. Perhaps, the boy did do it. I don't know, but I just don't believe it. So what?"[432]

Still, the potential implications of arresting of a Black man for the murder and rumored rape of a young white woman were not lost on the white-run papers. Harry N. Rickey, the former editor-in-chief of the Scripps Howard newspapers, wrote in an editorial for the Asheville paper:

> *I was keenly interested in the Clevenger murder case, because in my active newspaper career, I worked along with detectives and reporters many cases of similar character.…It seemed to me that the killer was a sex degenerate and a white man, probably on the young side. This was indicated by the mutilation of the girl's body as reported. From the first in theorizing about the crime, I eliminated the idea that it was committed by a colored man. But there seems to be no fixed pattern for murder.…The sane and calm way the people of Asheville have reacted to the news that a colored man is the murderer does not surprise me. I have known this community for about twenty years and would have been disappointed beyond words if it had gone off the deep end in an orgy of race hatred.…And in our thinking about this crime let us think in terms of the individual and not the race to which he happens to belong.*[433]

Despite the so-called "sane and calm way the people of Asheville… reacted," Sheriff Brown locked Martin Moore alone on an upper floor of the courthouse, suspended elevator service and canceled visiting hours—allowing no outside people into the building to circumvent any attempts at violence from a lynch mob.[434] Having publicized his plan to protect Moore, Brown also told the press that he was certain that Martin Moore lied about his motive. "He went there not to rob her, but to criminally assault her.…It is quite possible that after leaving the locker room the negro paused on the back stairway which he admitted using to reach the second floor, to watch Miss Clevenger through the window of her room. A clear view can be obtained without difficulty from this stairway." The Asheville papers led with Brown's accusation of rape.[435]

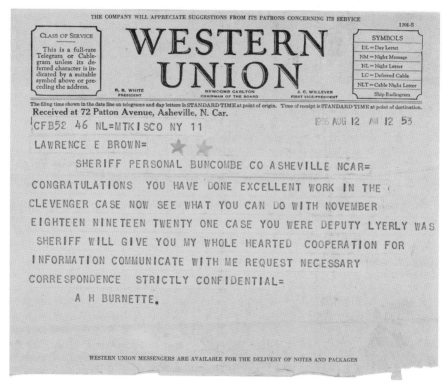

The November 18, 1921 case that A.H. Burnette refers to was the conviction of Rastus Burnett of first-degree murder for shooting his father-in-law, Richard W. Hare, while the two were working as rangers on George Vanderbilt's Biltmore Estate in Asheville. Shortly after the murder, the sheriff's department raided the Hare home and found a seventy-five-gallon copper still in the woods, as well as forty-six gallons of moonshine buried in the ground or concealed in hollow logs. *Laurence Brown Collection, Swannanoa Valley Museum & History Center, Black Mountain, North Carolina.*

Hundreds of people continued to gather at the courthouse hoping for a glimpse of the prisoner or the arresting detectives, and talk of a lynch mob persisted. Brown even received a phone call from London, England's the *Globe*, looking to verify a report that a "mob was storming the Buncombe county jail trying to get to Martin Moore." Sheriff Brown assured the reporter that this was not the case.[436]

With Martin Moore secured in the jail, Brown sat on his desk and sighed, "Maybe I can have a few minutes of rest now."[437] He left Asheville for respite at his home in Black Mountain. Here, his telephone rang almost nonstop with calls from around the country, congratulating him for his spectacular work in solving the case. Those who could not reach him by phone sent telegrams.[438] More publicly, prominent men in Asheville society praised Sheriff Brown in print, including the president of the chamber of commerce; the leaders of the local Rotary, Lions and Optimists Clubs; school and bank presidents; and prominent ministers. If the publicity was any indication, it seemed that Sheriff Brown's reelection was all but guaranteed. But Brown still needed to secure a conviction before the polls opened in November.[439]

"The grand jury and the solicitor can have him," Sheriff Brown said when reporters asked if he would press Moore on the details of his confession that did not match with the eyewitness version of events. "He's the murderer," Brown replied. "That's all we wanted to know."[440]

With the press and the public's interest in Helen's murder reignited, Martin Moore, still without a lawyer present or assigned, waived a preliminary hearing and was charged with first-degree murder and first-degree burglary; the penalty for conviction on either charge was death.[441]

Solicitor Zebulon Vance Nettles, who had been present at the confession and reenactment and would prosecute Moore, announced that the trial would begin at the next criminal term of superior court on August 17—just one week later.[442]

MOORE CONTINUED TO BE held at the county courthouse, and though Sheriff Brown refused to allow visitors into the building,[443] he did give photographers and reporters access to Moore,[444] who "peered dull-eyed from the barred window" overlooking "the mist-blue mountains." From outside the courthouse, Moore's "stone-ledged window looked like that of a medieval castle tower."[445]

The sheriff unlocked Martin's cell door for a "photo op." One staff correspondent for a Charlotte, North Carolina paper observed, "Moore

Sheriff Laurence Brown escorts a handcuffed Martin Moore through the jail, August 1936. *Author's collection.*

shambled out into the jail corridor and faced a small group of men....His eyes red with lack of sleep, his manner dejected."[446] Martin raised his cuffed hands to touch a phrase written above the cell door. An earlier occupant had scrawled, "The wages of sin is death" in big block letters. A photographer snapped a picture as Martin appeared to contemplate the verse. "He seemed eager to please the photographers who flashed lights into his eyes.

He borrowed a cigarette and sat down, turned sidewise and stood up in obedience to requests."[447]

Martin "appeared very nervous and ill at ease" and complained of not being able to sleep. He answered questions "freely, if slowly," telling the group solemnly, "I didn't mean to do nothing but look in the rooms for what I could find. I saw the white girl a time or two in the lobby but didn't know where she was rooming." In reply to a follow-up question about whether he was afraid during the search for Helen's killer, Martin said, "I worked on in the hotel and often passed right by the room. Everybody talked about it but I didn't say anything."[448]

He ducked his head to reenter the sparse cell. The bars were covered in years of dirt and grime; the metal bunks, with no mattresses, were bolted to the wall, the floors cement. The barred door slid closed.[449] Martin passed the time reading "an adventure and mystery story."[450]

Finally, on August 10, more than twenty-four hours after his confession, the judge, F. Donald Phillips, appointed Thomas A. Jones Jr., a local defense attorney, to represent Moore in court. Jones told reporters, "I will see that my client gets an absolutely fair trial. I have not yet had sufficient opportunity, or sufficient time in which to thoroughly investigate the facts. I was only appointed this morning and therefore am not in a position to state what lines the defense will take."[451]

At the same time, Dr. Mark Griffin, a local "well-known authority on nervous disease," paid a visit to Martin's cell block. Dr. Griffin, who had witnessed the reenactment, told Martin that he was there to decide whether the young man was fit to stand trial.

Martin removed his clothes, and Griffin began the cursory medical examination, listening to the taller man's heart and checking his ears and throat. He began with questions about Martin's health—was he sick? Had he ever had a disease? But he quickly moved on to bigger topics.

"Do you believe in Heaven or Hell?" Dr. Griffin began.

"I believe in part of it," Martin replied.

"If you were to die, where do you think that you would go?"

"Hell," Martin said.

"Did you kill Helen Clevenger?"

"No."[452]

THE FOLLOWING DAY, THE judge added another lawyer, J. Scroop Styles, to the defense. Styles quickly explained that he was only defending Moore "as a duty impressed on [him] by the court."[453] When asked for comment on a possible insanity plea, Styles replied that as he was just assigned to the case he had not had a chance to go "into this phase of the case with Mr. Jones,"[454] who could not be reached for comment. Styles shot down reporters' suggestions that the defense might not have time to make a genuine case for Moore's innocence with just a week to prepare. "We will be ready for trial next week," Styles replied.[455]

Dr. Griffin returned to Martin's cell to draw the young man's blood. The jailer brought Martin out of his cell. He perched on the radiator, framed by the window behind him. Dr. Griffin took a seat on a chair about seven feet away. Behind him stood Deputy A.Z. Bridgewater, the radio technician for the sheriff's department.

After asking how Martin felt, he asked again, "Did you kill Miss Clevenger?"

"Yes, sir, I killed her," Martin replied.

"You told me yesterday that you did not kill her."

"No, I told you that because I did not know who you were." Martin had since learned that Dr. Griffin was "a man sent up by…[Sheriff] Brown." He proceeded to obediently retell the story from his signed confession. Neither of his lawyers were present for either examination by the doctor.

Dr. Griffin finished his assessment of Moore, diagnosing him as being of "low intelligence" but "mentally sound" to stand trial later that week.[456]

Alongside news of Moore's impending trial were articles from the Associated Press out of Kentucky, reporting on the public hanging of Rainey Bethea, a twenty-two-year-old Black man convicted of the rape and murder of a seventy-year-old white woman. Bethea had confessed but later recanted his confession. The story was particularly newsworthy because the person typically charged with "springing the trap" and sending the accused to their death was the sheriff, which at that time was Florence Thompson, a woman. At the last minute, Thompson "lost her nerve" and deputized a former policeman known as "Dare Devil Dick" to be the executioner. A minute later, Bethea dropped to his death, and the crowd of fifteen thousand men, women and children cheered and yelled while munching on hot dogs and popcorn sold by vendors.[457]

Judge Phillips knew that Moore's trial would likely draw a similar carnival crowd. In preparation for the trial, he began to set regulations in place. The courtroom would be limited to a seating capacity of slightly over five hundred. No one would be allowed to stand. Attorneys and newspaper reporters would be assigned seats inside of the bar. Spectators would be given seats on the regular wooden benches in the order they arrived. Photographers would not be allowed to take pictures while the trial was in progress, only before the court convened, during recesses and after adjournment.[458]

"The taking of pictures in a courtroom when court is in session detracts from the dignity of the court," the judge told the reporters. "I have never allowed it and will not in this case."[459] Despite this proclamation, Ewart M. Ball, who photographed the reenactment, acted as the official court photographer and would also appear as a witness for the prosecution.[460] Judge Phillips refused a request to string telegraph wire into the courtroom but allowed the swarm of reporters to wire an adjoining room.[461]

On Monday afternoon, August 17, Martin Moore, wearing a black shirt and white suspenders fastened to dark pants, entered the courtroom handcuffed to Deputy Love Gudger, who escorted him to a chair beside his lawyers. Moore stood and listened to prosecutor Zeb Nettles read the murder charge. He was to be tried only for murder so that—in case of a not guilty verdict—he could be tried again on the burglary charge.[462] When asked how he pled, Moore replied, "I am not guilty." This plea came as no surprise; it was the plea that was required for capital offenses at the time.[463]

By law, "a child under school age, not able to read or write" selected the jurors,"[464] so five-year-old Mary Lois placed her hand into the jury box and one by one drew 145 slips of paper. On each paper was the name of a man from Buncombe County, including "the names of many negroes."[465] According to the New York Daily News, "The names of a few colored folk were placed in the box, so that constitutional objection could not be raised."[466] Court officials were particularly wary of maintaining the appearance of a fair and impartial trial. Just months before, the U.S. Supreme Court had overturned the Scottsboro Boys' guilty verdict when they found that African Americans had been systematically excluded from the jury rolls.[467]

Moore watched intently, his chin cupped in his hand, as the small girl drew each white paper.[468] The potential jurors were summoned to appear at the courthouse two days later.[469]

Scores of people desperately phoned the clerk of court attempting to reserve seats to watch the trial, even calling the deputy clerk at home. Ultimately, the rule was "first come, first served"[470] and by 6:00 a.m. the day of the trial, spectators had already begun gathering at the courthouse. Two and a half hours later, all seats had been filled, and despite the judge's earlier contention that no standing would be allowed, people crowded in around

Martin Moore sits behind one of his lawyers in the Buncombe County Superior Courtroom, Asheville, August 1936. *E.M. Ball Photographic Collection, D.H. Ramsey Library Special Collections, UNC–Asheville, 28804.*

the perimeter of the courtroom, flowing out into the hallways. Spectators scavenged chairs from unoccupied offices. By the time court was in session, hundreds of people had been turned away. Black people in attendance were segregated into the courtroom's small balcony.[471]

Jury selection began. Of the 145 names drawn, which included the court photographer and Ed Frady, a hotel employee and witness, only one belonged to a Black man—M.L. Bost. Bost arrived at the courthouse with a certificate from his doctor stating that he was physically unable to serve due to a leg injury. Bost was one of ten potential jurors excused.[472]

Bost and his doctor, a prominent Black member of the local Interracial Commission, likely knew that serving on the jury would be dangerous for Bost. They were not wrong. A little over two years later, another Black man, Lawrence Sigmon, was summoned by the sheriff for jury duty. When he arrived at the courthouse, several deputies "carried him to an elevator…stopped [the car] between floors" and "severely" beat him. Sigmon said that the deputies

Doctor's note excusing M.L. Bost from serving on Martin Moore's jury, August 19, 1936. *State Archives of North Carolina.*

told him he was being made "an example for all other Asheville Negroes who might have the audacity to report when summoned for jury duty." Sigmon was then charged with disorderly conduct and sentenced to three months of hard labor on a chain gang. The National Association for the Advancement of Colored People (NAACP) intervened, and the charges were dropped.[473]

From the remaining pool of white men, the deputy clerk's eight-year-old son drew names over a nearly five-hour morning session. Twelve men would be selected to make up the official jury, with a thirteenth to serve as an alternate "in case one of the others [was] incapacitated."[474]

Each juror drawn from the box was questioned by the prosecution and defense. They were asked about their prior knowledge of the case and whether they could deliver a "fair and impartial" verdict. At least seven were excused because they did not believe in capital punishment and three others because they thought Moore was guilty.

But when Cecil Bishop, a thirty-two-year-old farmer from Fairview, "expressed an opinion that the negro was guilty," Judge Phillips still added

Bishop to the jury, overruling objections from Moore's defense team. Another man, John Hursey, told the court that he had formed a "casual" opinion about Moore's guilt but that "evidence could remove that opinion." He too was seated on the jury.[475]

Moore leaned forward in his chair and studied the faces of the jurors intently.

As the selection continued, Solicitor Nettles noticed with frustration a new face seated in front of Moore at the defense table—Asheville attorney Sanford W. Brown (no relation to the sheriff).

"The state has a right to demand of Mr. Brown to name the person he is representing, if he is in this trial as counsel," Nettles told the judge.

Brown replied that he had just been hired by Martin Moore's sister. Judge Phillips initially told the attorney he would not be allowed to represent Moore but quickly reversed his decision, allowing Sanford Brown to stay. Immediately, Scroop Styles stood and "created a flurry" when he asked to be excused from his court-appointed duty. The judge denied his request.

W.G. Hamilton *(far right)* consults with one of the lawyers representing Martin Moore. Moore is seated behind them. The Battery Park Hotel can be seen out the window at right, August 1936. *E.M. Ball Photographic Collection, D.H. Ramsey Library Special Collections, UNC–Asheville, 28804.*

Martin would be represented by three lawyers—Thomas Jones, Scroop Styles and Sanford Brown.[476]

The other new face at the polished wooden defense table was attorney W.G. Hamilton, the only other Black person not seated in the balcony besides Martin and his sister. His presence was not questioned by Nettles or the judge. Hamilton told the reporters sitting nearby that Moore's family had requested that he "act in an advisory capacity."[477]

After examining forty-five potential jurors, twelve white men, "most of whom said they had daughters,"[478] were tasked with deciding Martin Moore's fate. They were "four farmers, a coal dealer, two bleachery employees, a jewelry store proprietor, a retired department store executive, a butcher, a tailor, and an engineer."[479]

It was a hot mid-August day. Those who chanced vacating their seats for lunch came back carrying paper fans. Others fanned themselves with their hats. A court official passed out visors to the jurors to shield them from the sun pouring through the large plate glass windows directly opposite the jury box. When the glare cleared, the thirteen men had a clear view of the Battery Park Hotel towering over the city.[480]

At 3:15 p.m., the state called William Clevenger as the first witness. William repeated, almost exactly, the story he had already told investigators about his travels with his niece and his discovery of her body.[481] William and his brother, Clinton, were the only members of Helen's family in the courtroom for the first day of the trial.[482]

Throughout the testimonies, Moore sat hunched over the table, his hands folded in front of him.[483] Despite the *Asheville Citizen* headline the next morning, "State's Witnesses Link Moore with Slaying," none of the state's early witnesses directly tied Moore to the murder.

Instead, the prosecution's aim during the trial's first day was to provide the jury a general picture of Helen's life and the uncontested facts of her death. The defense remained mostly silent, making few objections.

By the end of the day, the defense had crossed-examined only one witness, manager Pat Branch.

"Isn't it possible there at the hotel a person who is not a guest could enter during the daytime, conceal himself somewhere in that hotel?" Thomas Jones asked of Branch.[484]

"It might be possible," Branch replied.

"Do you know the defendant, Martin Moore?" Jones continued.

William Clevenger sits in the courtroom as spectators crowd behind him. *E.M. Ball Photographic Collection, D.H. Ramsey Library Special Collections, UNC–Asheville, 28804.*

"Yes."

"How long have you known him?"

"He has been in the employ of the hotel about two and a half years." Branch said.

"Do you know his general reputation?"

"Yes, it is good," Branch concluded.[485] Jones sat back down. Solicitor Nettles was allowed to reexamine Branch for the prosecution.

"I will ask you if you are not testifying that Martin Moore has a good character for the reason that you are afraid you might be sued…in a civil action?" Solicitor Nettles queried Branch, his voice rising.

"I would say that any employee that has worked in your hotel, and you have been associated with him and seen him working for two and one-half years, and he has never given you any trouble, and you have never heard anything against him, ought to be a pretty good man." Branch replied.[486]

The court recessed for the day after less than two hours, and reporters left mostly disappointed with the lack of new information to wire into their papers.

Carpenter A.H. "Slim" Tomberlin explains a model he made of the second floor of the Battery Park Hotel, showing Helen's room in three dimensions, August 1936. *E.M. Ball Photographic Collection, D.H. Ramsey Library Special Collections, UNC–Asheville, 28804.*

The jurors were sequestered overnight. Though they were allowed magazines and newspapers, the deputy sheriff in charge of keeping them together was instructed to remove any coverage of the murder or court case.[487]

THE GOSSIP MILL IN Asheville was as active as ever. A reporter for the *Burlington (NC) Daily Times-News* wrote: "In the hotel lobby, in the cafes, on the streets, natives would talk cautiously, then throw up a defense barrier of, 'I don't know. It all is such a mystery!' They fear possible questioning, even now, and yet they have misgivings and grave doubts. They do not call names."[488]

The trial continued to attract more spectators than the courtroom could hold, and the late summer weather combined with the number of bodies packed into the room produced sweltering temperatures. "Lady, here's a fan. If you're going to the courtroom, you'll need it," one of the elevator operators told a woman as he handed out paper fans with advertisements printed on them, provided by an enterprising merchant.[489]

People would not be turned away. Another spectator, tired of standing, asked a courthouse employee for a chair. When she was refused, she angrily replied, "Well, something has to be done. I'm sick and I can't stand up during the trial."[490]

While Moore's defense team had remained fairly inert the first day, as the trial entered its second day, they rallied. Just after court was called into session, the defense attempted to block the state from introducing any ballistic evidence. They argued that the pistol found under Moore's house, in particular, should not be considered because "the officers had no right to take charge of the negro, they had no reasonable grounds to believe he had committed a felony, and they obtained the weapon in violation of his rights as provided in the fourth and fifth amendments to the constitution."[491] The judge quickly overruled the objection.[492]

Deputy Tom Brown, his hat in hand, ambled up to the witness stand to identify the gun as the one he found under Martin Moore's porch.[493] Solicitor Nettles then called a young clerk from Uncle Sam's Loan Office, a pawn shop in Asheville. The clerk, Emanuel Hirsch, kept the books for the shop and brought records to trial showing that the gun in question had been in the shop's inventory earlier that year. Another Uncle Sam's employee then testified that he sold Martin the same weapon and ammunition. He explained that Martin had traded another pistol, which Moore told him had been thrown out a neighbor's window during a police raid, for the .32-caliber automatic.[494]

But just days before, Asheville's newspapers, alongside the text of Moore's signed confession, had reported on investigations into the weapon. When detectives visited Uncle Sam's, the owner, Sam Argintar, told them that Moore had not purchased a pistol from the shop. And the bullets used to kill Helen were an "outlaw" brand, which according to Argintar, the shop did not sell. Argintar was not called to the stand, and the defense did not cross examine either of the pawn shop clerks.[495]

The prosecution then called New York Police sergeant Harry Butts. Butts was "an expert who had fired more than 200,000 test shots from various weapons and who was familiar with all types of pistols." He testified that he had extensively examined the pistol found under Martin's house, the exploded shell found in Helen's bathroom, the bullet pulled from her body and three unfired cartridges taken from the magazine of Moore's weapon. Butts first explained to the jury how bullets can be "positively identified" as being fired from a specific weapon based on markings the firing pin made on the shell.[496] While rifling scratches left behind on a bullet can link it back to a specific weapon, these markings can change every three to five shots.[497]

Prior to Moore's arrest, the *Asheville Citizen* had reported that "the bullet had no distinct rifling marks on it, meaning that it was fired from a barrel slightly too large for it. The theory that the barrel was a bit larger than the bullet was supported by the fact that the bullet did not go entirely through Miss Clevenger's body."[498]

But Butts testified that "some of the peculiar markings on the bullets [Butts] fired from the gun…were caused by the barrel of the weapon being split" and showed the split barrel to the jury. All but one of the men left the jury box to get a closer look.[499]

Butts explained that the pistol "jammed" twice when he fired "six or eight" test bullets. The jam was caused by the bullets failing to feed from the magazine into the barrel. Every time the gun jammed, "it made an indentation on the side of the brass shell and scratched the nose of the steel-jacketed bullet."[500] The gun "jamming" supported Sheriff Brown's contention that the murderer beat Helen with the butt of the gun when he was unable to fire another shot. When examined under a microscope, Butts concluded, the test shot bullets had "markings identical with those on the bullet that ended the young girl's life."[501]

"Now," the prosecutor asked, "do you have an opinion as to what gun that bullet was fired from?"

"I do," the sergeant replied.

"What is it?"

"It was fired by that pistol."[502]


Harry Schwartz, first assistant toxicologist for the City of New York, who had performed chemical analysis on the weapon, testified for the state that there was human blood on the end of the pistol's clip and one small, "light colored" human hair. Days earlier, the *Asheville Times* had reported that investigators were "expected to type the blood on the cartridge clip and to compare it with a sample of Miss Clevenger's blood," but either this was not done or there was not a match, as Helen's blood type was not brought up at trial. Forensic science at the time was unable to provide more detailed information on the source of the blood or hair, and the prosecutor did not ask Schwartz to wager a guess or give an opinion.[503]

For their part, the defense, led by J. Scroop Styles, tried. The *Charlotte Observer* reported, "Objections, which Judge Nettles over-ruled consistently, punctured

Erwin Pittman testifies for the State, August 1936. *E.M. Ball Photographic Collection, D.H. Ramsey Library Special Collections, UNC–Asheville, 28804.*

almost every question of Solicitor Nettles."[504] Still, if they did cross-examine any of the state's ballistic and forensic witnesses, it was not reported in the papers.

Nearing the end of the trial's second day, Erwin Pittman shared his eyewitness testimony. Pittman told jurors that after hearing "three to five screams," he opened his door, saw a figure standing in the threshold of Helen's room and said, "I wonder what that noise was? It sounded as if someone were in pain." Now under oath, Pittman told the court that a man's voice replied, "That's what I was wondering myself."

The defense chose not to cross-examine.[505]

THE TRIAL TOOK ITS first dramatic turn soon after Sheriff Brown swore his oath and sat in the witness box. As he finished relating the expected information—how he found Helen's body, the state of her room and Moore's arrest—Solicitor Nettles asked, "Did you talk to the defendant, Moore?"[506]

Before the sheriff could answer, the three defense attorneys, Styles, Jones and Sanford Brown, stood together and said in unison, "We object, your honor." Judge Phillips ordered the jury from the room while the crowd excitedly watched. Styles insisted that Moore's signed confession could not be introduced as evidence, as it had been obtained under duress and promises of leniency by the sheriff.[507]

According to the *Charlotte Observer*, "Everyone had expected this motion. Sheriff Brown expected it. You could see it from the way he smiled." Solicitor Nettles questioned the sheriff. Was the confession made voluntarily? Brown answered in "clipped sentences. He had promised the negro nothing. He had not used duress to get the statement." Maintaining consistent eye contact and with a grim expression,[508] Sheriff Brown told the jury, "The only thing I said, that if he told me the truth I would tell the judge that he did tell me the truth about it, and possibly it might help him. That is all I ever told him."[509]

The judge sustained the motion, a major but short-lived win for the defense, as Judge Phillips then ruled the confession that Martin had made to Dr. Griffin and Deputy Bridgewater while in jail as admissible. The jury returned.[510] But even without the later confession, everyone in the courtroom, the men on the jury included, had likely already read the confession in full when it was published in newspapers across the country—including on the front page of the best-selling extra edition of the *Asheville Citizen-Times*.[511]

Bridgewater came to the stand and told the same story from Moore's signed and published confession. Dr. Griffin affirmed his statements.

"What did he tell you with reference to shooting her with a pistol?" Nettles asked.

"He told me that he shot her," Griffin replied.

"Did you offer him any reward…or promise him anything for talking to you there?" the solicitor queried.

"No, sir."[512]

The defense cross-examined Dr. Griffin. The jury heard that during his medical evaluation of Moore, Griffin had found several "discolorations" on Moore's body, including "bruises on his arms, a discoloration below his left eye, and another on his left shoulder."[513]

These discolorations would become a significant piece of evidence when, the following morning only fourteen minutes after court was called to order, the state rested and the defense began to call witnesses.[514]

# 10

# A LIBERAL APPLICATION
# OF RUBBER HOSE

Martin Moore, wearing a light blue shirt, a change from the black shirt he had worn the past two days, made his way across the tiled courtroom floor, passing directly in front of the jury. He laid his hand on a Bible, swearing to tell the truth.

"Many spectators sat on the edge of their seats in order to get a better view. A number sat up on the arms of their chairs and some even stood," the *Asheville Citizen* reported. Finally, an officer yelled, "Everybody that has a seat sit down."[515]

This was the first day that Helen's father, Joseph, attended the trial. But when Martin took the stand, Joseph got to his feet and "walked unsteadily toward a door at the rear of the courtroom."[516] Reporters hurriedly followed, jumping over the bannister separating the press table from the general public.[517]

"Mr. Sheriff, the next time anyone climbs like a monkey over the bench, please arrest him," Judge Phillips called after the retreating reporters.[518]

By the time Joseph reached the hallway, his eyes were "glassy" and he began to sway. Attempting to steady himself, he grabbed the door frame to the court stenographer's office. Two men offered Joseph their arms. They assisted the grieving father to a chair and positioned an electric fan in front of him, turning it on. Joseph sat hunched over, his head in his hands, trying to catch his breath. Recovering, he went to his hotel to rest, in hopes that he would be able to testify on behalf of his daughter before the end of the trial.[519]

With Joseph Clevenger out of the room, Sanford Brown began questioning Martin. Brown began by trying to establish that though Martin did own a gun he had loaned it to L.D. Roddy the day before the murder and that when Roddy returned it, the day after the murder, the gun had a "stain" on it.[520]

"Why did you not give the gun to the officers?" Sanford Brown asked.

"I was scared to for fear they would put it on me." Moore replied. He then explained to the jury that "after [Tom Brown] found the gun, [the officers said] 'this gun has got blood and hair on it.'... They brought me to the hotel, and then over to [room] 509, in the [courthouse]."

Helen's father, Joseph Clevenger, attends her funeral in Fletcher, Ohio, on July 22, 1936. *ACME Newspictures, author's collection.*

"What else, if anything, was done to you?" his attorney queried.

"Mr. [Laurence] Brown...said, you go back in that room, it won't be no picnic if you go back there. You had better come to my office and talk to me alone. Mr. Tom [Brown] carried me back in his office and they started whipping me," Martin said.

"Who whipped you?"

"Mr. Tom and two New York detectives."

"What with?"

"A hose," Martin said as murmurs rose among the spectators.[521]

THIS APPEARED TO BE the first the jury had heard of the confession being beaten from Martin Moore. And if they had been reading the white-owned newspaper coverage prior to their sequestration, they would have seen nothing but praise for the detectives who secured Moore's confession.

"It was a wonderful piece of detective work," New York Police commissioner Lewis Joseph Valentine said as he shook the New York detectives' hands when they arrived back in the city. "Good, hard work of this type should be an example to the entire force. In this case both intellectual work and the strain of grilling the suspect continuously for fifty-one hours had to be taken into account."[522] Fifty-one hours? Perhaps

Detectives Thomas Martin (*second from left*) and John Quinn (*second from right*) receive commendation from New York police commissioner Lewis Valentine (*far left*). *Author's collection.*

Valentine was mistakenly referring to the time elapsed between the arrival of the detectives from New York and Moore's confession, which was obtained after "only" six hours of "grilling."

A week after the commendation was published in the *New York Times*, the *New York Amsterdam News*, a prominent Black-run newspaper, published Harlem resident Ethelred Brown's letter to the editor mocking Commissioner Valentine's praise of the detectives. "Great Detective Work?...I think I could myself have forced a confession from the frightened southern Negro in about twelve hours; and I am sure that by the use of the well known New York police method of two good resounding socks on the jaw fifty hours of valuable time could have been saved....I have just read that the confession, according to Moore, was obtained in the usual New York manner by a liberal application of rubber hose. What a wonderful piece of detective work!"[523]

The allegation of beating likely did not come as a surprise to many. The use of violence and threats by law enforcement officials to obtain confessions was a widespread and common practice in most parts of the United States according to a 1931 report published by the Wickersham Commission on Law Observance and Enforcement. This report excluded the Southeast, but the region had numerous documented cases. In *Brown v. Mississippi*, for example, three Black men confessed to the murder of a white farmer after police beatings. They were convicted. An appeal went to the U.S. Supreme Court in February 1936, just five months before Helen's murder. The high court overturned the verdict and ruled that coerced confessions could not be used as evidence in court.[524]

Still, by 1940, the practice had become so rampantly used against Black men and boys as to be a stereotype. Richard Wright, acclaimed author of *Native Son*, wrote in an essay that year:

> *Any Negro who has lived in the North or the South knows that times without number he has heard of some Negro boy being picked up on the streets and carted off to jail and charged with "rape." This thing happens so often that to my mind it had become a representative symbol of the Negro's uncertain position in America. Let me describe this stereotyped situation: A crime wave is sweeping a city and citizens are clamoring for police action. Squad cars cruise the Black Belt and grab the first Negro boy who seems to be unattached and homeless. He is held for perhaps a week without charge or bail, without the privilege of communicating with anyone, including his own relatives. After a few days this boy "confessed" anything that he is asked to confess, any crime that handily happens to be unsolved and on the calendar. Why does he confess? After the boy has been grilled night and day, hanged up by his thumbs, dangled by his feet out the twenty-story windows, and beaten (in places that leave no scars—cops have found a way to do that), he signs the papers before him, papers which are usually accompanied by a verbal promise to the boy that he will not go to the electric chair....Indeed, scarcely was* Native Son *off the press before Supreme Court Justice Hugo L. Black gave the nation a long and vivid account of the American police methods of handling Negro boys.*[525]

In 1937, Hugo Black, a U.S. senator from Alabama and former member of the Ku Klux Klan, became Franklin Delano Roosevelt's first appointment to the U.S. Supreme Court. Just three years later, in a dramatic turn from his Klan days, Black wrote the majority opinion that Richard Wright refers to in his essay. While still touting racist ideas of while supremacy, the decision nullified the conviction of four Black men who confessed to the murder of a white man after police used "third degree" tactics, including beatings, torture, withholding food and sleep and refusing access to a lawyer. The decision went on to outlaw all third-degree interrogation tactics and note that these tactics overwhelmingly were being used against Black men, their convictions and death penalty sentences handed down by all-white juries.[526]


"HOW MANY TIMES DID they strike you?" attorney Sanford Brown asked Moore as the young man sat with his hands folded in his lap.

"I could not count them."

"Where were you being hit at?"

"Across my chest, back, and arm," Martin indicated the spots on his long torso.

"Describe the hose that they used."

"It was about two feet long," Moore said, holding his hands in front of him.

"Which wielded the hose on you?"

"Mr. [Tom] Brown whipped me a while with it, and then the New York detective whipped me, and then the other whipped me," Moore said, not taking his eyes from his lawyer.

"While they were whipping you, did they ask you questions?"

"They asked me if I would tell that I killed Miss Clevenger," Martin responded.

"What did you say to that?"

"I said I did not do it."

"How long did that go on?" Brown asked.

"It went on for about 20 minutes."

"Did they hit you with anything else except the hose?"

"The big fat New York detective [John Quinn] hit me in the stomach with his fist," Moore replied.

"After they whipped you what was done with you?"

"This New York detective took me in the other room adjoining 509. He took me and talked to me. He said to tell him and he would not let them whip me any more."

"After carrying you there what was done?" pressed the defense attorney.

"He said, 'We will let you three boys [Martin Moore, Banks Taylor and L.D. Roddy] get by yourselves and decide which one had the gun,' so they brought us out in the courtroom from that office and we sat over there. I was handcuffed to Banks Taylor, so we sat there. I asked L.D. didn't he have my gun and he said, 'Naw,' so we sat there for half an hour and after while they came and got Banks and carried him out."

"What was said, if anything, about having finger prints or blood stains?" Sanford Brown asked.

"The big fat detective from New York came in there and said, 'We found the finger prints on the lampshade, and it was yours.'"

"Who was he directing that to?"

"He pointed to me. I told him that I had not been in that room. Then he said, 'I am going to beat you until you tell,' or 'I am going to beat you to death,'" said Martin.

"What did they do?"

"Then they started whipping me."

"Again."

"Yes," Martin confirmed.

"How long did that continue?"

"He hit me five licks and I said I would talk."

"Why did you talk?"

"Because they said that they had enough evidence to prove that I did it, and they were going to whip me again," Martin explained.

"What was done to you after you said that you would talk?"

"They sat me down there and they wrote out half of what I told them, and helped me explain it, and told me what to say, that I went in there to take some money."

"Did you sign any statement?"

"Yes, sir. I signed it."[527]

Later in the day, the jury heard from several witnesses corroborating Martin Moore's testimony. C.B. Callahan, the courthouse janitor, said that a two-foot piece of rubber hose was missing when he came in to work the day after Moore signed his confession. He had left the hose in the bathroom on the fifth floor of the courthouse, the same floor on which Moore had just testified that Deputy Tom Brown and the New York detectives had whipped him with a rubber hose. Callahan had not seen the length of hose since.[528]

And two doctors hired by the defense testified that they examined Moore three days after his confession and found several bruises on his left forearm, upper arm and shoulder.[529]

Sanford Brown then proceeded to question Moore about the confession he made to Dr. Griffin. Martin admitted that he confessed to Griffin but only because he "thought that he would tell Sheriff Brown and…that Sheriff Brown was going to keep his promise" of leniency.[530]

WITH THE ALLEGATIONS OF beating and coercion now in front of the jury, the defense set to establishing Martin's alibi.

"Martin, where were you on the night Miss Clevenger was killed?" Sanford Brown asked.

"I was over at Fannie Lee's house,"[531] Moore said easily, referring to his girlfriend of three years, Fannie Lee Gilliam.[532] He arrived at her home between 8:30 and 9:00 p.m.

"Who was there?" said Brown.

Martin hesitated, thinking. After a beat he said, "Well, I was in the kitchen and there was Fannie and Alma and her brother."

"Were there any other people there?"

"Yes, but I did not want to go in the front room. I only went as far as the kitchen at that time. I stayed there until around a quarter of ten, then I started to leave and Fannie Lee come as far as the yard with me, so me and her stood and talked five or ten minutes, until Gene Williams and his wife, Virgie, came along. She said, 'Come and go back to the house.' I went to the kitchen with them, and stayed around the kitchen for ten or fifteen minutes. I told her I was feeling bad, and I believed I would go home. She said, 'You can lay down across my—'"

Solicitor Nettles interrupted with an objection. The judge asked, "In consequence of what she said, what did you do?"

"I did not go home. I went and laid down on the bed."

"How long did you stay there?"

"When I woke up her clock was five minutes to two."

"What did you do then?" asked the defense attorney.

"I got up and went home."[533]

Fannie Lee later testified that she was "sure of the date Moore was at her home because it was her birthday and she was having a party."[534] The *Asheville Citizen* allowed only one paragraph of coverage for Gilliam's testimony at the end of an article on page seven of the daily paper.[535]

Several other people who were at Fannie Lee's party also spoke in Moore's defense, including Gene and Virgie Williams. Gene confirmed that both he and Moore were at the party. During cross-examination, the prosecution noted that Gene had been in prison for robbery and indicted for reckless and intoxicated driving. Likewise, Gene's wife remembered seeing and talking to Martin around 10:15 p.m. at the party, during the time the prosecution said Moore was reading a novel in the locker room of the Battery Park Hotel. Under cross-examination, the prosecutor emphasized that Virgie had two liquor law violations on her record.

The Williamses' employer confirmed that he had overheard the couple discussing Moore's presence at the party when they first heard their friend had been arrested.[536]

AFTER LESS THAN AN hour, Moore finished testifying in his own defense. For the next two hours, Solicitor Nettles cross-examined him.

Nettles began by reading from the transcript of the reenactment prepared by the court stenographer, asking Moore after each point in the statement if that was what he had told the investigators. Moore gave short answers to each query, saying, "Yes" or "That is right" or "That is what I told you." The prosecutor's questions came more and more rapidly.

By the *Asheville Citizen*'s account, Solicitor Nettles "scored heavily" during his cross-examination. The paper reported, "Several times the defendant made positive statements that directly connected him with the crime." The transcript of the exchange between Nettles and Moore, however, revealed a young man who was tired and confused after nearly three straight hours of questioning, primarily by the prosecutor who shouted and shook his finger in Martin's face as he made his "ceaseless" accusations in front of a room full of hundreds of people.[537]

A reporter for the *Citizen* wrote, "Preparing a 'trap' for the negro," Nettles asked, "This is your pistol?"

"Yes," Martin replied.

"The same pistol that had the blood on it?"

"Yes."

"The same pistol you hid under your toilet?"

"Yes."

"The same one you showed us that you had in your britches that night when you went into that hotel?"

"Yes, the same one," Moore answered as "an audible ripple of surprise went through the audience."

The *Asheville Citizen* continued its analysis of the cross-examination, reporting, "It was apparent that the negro did not realize he was making unqualified statements at these times since he was careful on other occasions to say the statements he was making were those he had confessed to because of fear and that they were not true. When he drew Moore into making these statements Solicitor Nettles did not question him further about them, leaving the negro in the apparent belief he had not damaged himself."[538]

Solicitor Zeb V. Nettles, August 1936. *E.M. Ball Photographic Collection, D.H. Ramsey Library Special Collections, UNC–Asheville, 28804.*

KEY TO THE DEFENSE'S strategy was proving that Martin did not have a gun in his possession the night of the murder. But beyond Martin's own testimony that he had lent his pistol to L.D. Roddy, the defense called no witnesses to corroborate his story.[539]

A few days before the trial began, Moore's legal team had submitted an affidavit demanding that they be allowed to interview Roddy and Banks Taylor. Both Roddy and Taylor had been sitting in jail since Martin's

Martin Moore follows Deputy Love Gudger from the courtroom, August 1936. *E.M. Ball Photographic Collection, D.H. Ramsey Library Special Collections, UNC–Asheville, 28804.*

arrest, held without bond. They both knew the sheriff was considering charging them with accessory after the fact for not reporting that Martin Moore owned a gun.[540]

The defense attorneys had "information that L.D. Roddy and Banks Taylor knew certain facts that were material to the defense of [Martin

Moore]," but when Styles and Jones went to the jail, Sheriff Brown and Solicitor Nettles refused to let them in to see or talk to the men.[541]

Roddy did eventually take the stand, but for the prosecution as their first rebuttal witness. Besides denying that he borrowed Martin's gun, Roddy told the court that he was in the next room when the officers questioned Martin and saw no sign of abuse.[542]

The last witness to testify that day, Walter B. Orr, the former Charlotte police chief, offered an alternate theory for where Moore got the "discolorations" on his body. He told the court that "Moore and Roddy got into a fight in the courthouse the morning the defendant was arrested" and that Orr had to separate the two after he heard Roddy say to Moore, "What you trying to do, get me lynched?"[543]

Banks Taylor did not testify.[544]


COURT OPENED ON THE trial's final day, and the defense team wrapped up their case for the jury with a statement from J. Scroop Styles, who reiterated that he was not defending Moore of his "own choice" but rather because the law mandated that anyone accused of a capital crime was guaranteed a lawyer.

"This negro is entitled to a fair and impartial trial and this is all in God's name we are asking of you gentlemen," Styles told the jury. "My heart goes out to the parents of this child who was slain while in our city. But regardless of our sentiment we must do our duty and defend this man. I wish to pay my respects to the solicitor. He has prosecuted this negro in an impartial manner. He has been most fair to us. I also wish to thank the officers who worked on this case. Regardless of who is guilty we wish to commend the officers."

Between his thinly veiled comments affirming his own feelings on the guilt of his client, Styles did stress that law enforcement entered Moore's home without a warrant, arrested and handcuffed him "without letting him know what he was charged with" and then refused him access to a lawyer for six hours as they questioned him. He argued that the officers knowingly "overstepped their authority" when they falsely told Moore that his fingerprints were on the pistol and the lampshade in Helen's room.[545]

"Why didn't they (the prosecution) bring (Detective) Quinn and (Deputy Sheriff) Tom Brown to deny Moore's testimony that they beat him?" Styles asked.[546]

He told the jury that it was obvious that the language from the written confessions was not Moore's.[547] And though the pistol did belong to

Martin Moore, the defense team "contended that the gun was not in Moore's hands" the night of the murder.[548]

"Why did this Roddy testify that he went home at 1 o'clock that morning and went into his kitchen? I'll tell you gentlemen, he went in there to wash the blood of this young girl from his hands," Styles argued.[549]

"The lethal gas chamber is too good for the man, Martin Moore or any other person, who committed this brutal crime," Styles continued. "I am not speaking for Martin Moore but for the two million or more citizens of the great state of North Carolina who say through their laws that officers can't walk into Martin Moore's home, take him away, mistreat him and then try him for his life. Your verdict must say that you stand by the officers in their enforcement of the criminal laws but you do not approve of the mistreatment of prisoners.

"If you are satisfied beyond a reasonable doubt that this negro is guilty then for God's sake say so. If you are not so satisfied then say so. Be careful in making up your decision so that when you are walking in the shadows of the setting sun you will hear Him say, 'Well done my good and faithful servant.'"[550]

For the next fifty-one minutes, Solicitor Zeb V. Nettles presented his closing argument in increasingly fervent tones.

"I will not attempt to appeal to your sympathy because Moore is a negro," Nettles began. "That poor little girl must have lived 10 years in a few moments on that dark and stormy night when that tall, big black man entered her room. I remind you again that she could have been your niece, wife or daughter....Now they are talking about mercy for that giant. For the same person who stole into that girl's room intent upon robbery or rape, I don't know which, and killed that little girl," he continued. "God only knows how this girl's poor grief-stricken mother feels now. Waiting at her home for the return of a daughter who will never return. All their lives the parents will wonder why God, in His great wisdom, struck down their little girl as she was about to enter up on life's work.

"I am not asking you to condemn the colored race. They have their place in this civilization. Let's not condemn the whole race. Let's put the man responsible for this crime where he belongs.

"In the name of womanhood, put this murderer and rapist in the gas chamber. He is a menace to society and as long as he walks the streets of our fair city your wife or daughter or your niece is in peril....You 12 men are responsible to your community, your country and to your God to render a true verdict in this case and I am asking you, as your solicitor, to return to this box and say that this Martin Moore is guilty as charged and must die."[551]

The jury began deliberations.[552]

While they were out of the room, spectators—including the wives of Sheriff Brown and Solicitor Nettles—crowded to the front of the courtroom to view the photographs exhibited during the trial more closely. Judge Phillips told the bailiff, "Arrest anybody who makes any disturbance in the courtroom."[553]

The crowd did not have long to wait. Fifty-six minutes later, the jury filed back into the courtroom. They had cast only one ballot to decide the case.

"Gentlemen of the jury, look upon the prisoner. Is he guilty of the felony and murder whereof he stands indicted, or not guilty?"

A hush went through the courtroom.

"Guilty of murder in the first degree."

Martin's sister, a slender woman clad in a light blue dress, began sobbing. Martin remained stoic. Helen's father "rubbed his pale cheek briskly."[554]

Sanford Brown stood. "We wish to make a motion to set aside the verdict as against the weight of the evidence."

"Denied," the judge answered immediately. "But I will hear from you gentlemen [of the defense] before I enter Judgement."

Styles began, "Mr. Brown wishes the usual appeal entries made, but speaking for Mr. Jones and myself…we did the very best we could. There is nothing now to be said on behalf of the defendant, which this jury has not already heard. This verdict carries but one sentence, and of course, it is the duty now of the court to pronounce that sentence. I wish to say for myself and Mr. Jones that we feel this has been a fair and impartial trial and we have nothing further to say. We ask the court now to relieve us from further duties in the case."

The judge considered the request. "You have represented this defendant in a most able manner. The court thanks you for that service. Mr. Brown, since you have been employed by members of the family after counsel had been appointed by the court, I think that Mr. Jones and Mr. Styles can now be relieved. Let Martin Moore stand here."

Martin "slowly raised his lank figure from his chair and, balancing himself with one…hand on a chair in front of him, his head drooped slightly."

"Martin Moore, have you anything to say to the court before the court pronounces the death sentence upon you in this case?"

"No, sir. I thanks the jury," Martin replied.[555]

"Martin, it is not the purpose to take your life for what you have done," Judge Phillips began. "If the law by punishing you can save another life, save some woman from being raped, save some house from being burned or broken into in the night, then the law has done something valuable to its citizenship. Therefore, to the people now listening, I want you to understand that the law has no animosity toward Martin Moore. The law is not demanding a pound of flesh from him. It is punishing Martin Moore in the first instance for what he has done, and secondly, more greatly, many times more greatly, it is punishing him for the purpose of warning others who want to do likewise."

The judge set the date of Martin's execution for October 2, 1936.[556]

Deputy Tom Brown handcuffed Moore and escorted him from the room into his brother's waiting armored car. As they left the building, the two men chatted about dice games. "I don't reckon I'll shoot any more craps," Martin told Tom, "but if I do, I guess I'll shoot a seven or eleven."[557]

They left Asheville heading east to Raleigh.[558] After a few hours of driving, the group stopped to grab sandwiches for dinner. Moore told the deputies, "Don't pay for them. Tell him to charge them to me and to collect from me personally on October 3."[559]

# I'VE WRITTEN TO MY BROTHER TO COME AND GET MY BODY.

All I know is that Martin was a good boy to me. I raised him, and even until the time he was arrested he minded me just like a little child," Martin's mother, Celie, told reporters after the trial. "Of course he ran around like all boys, but every pay day he always gave me half of his wages. If he done it he never told me. Only God and Martin know what is inside his breast."

The "feeble," "aged darky," who had been "sick since last February" and was "unsteady on her feet" only requested of officers that they return the clothing and belongings they had taken from Martin upon his arrest and "leave the rest to God."[560]

Martin's brother, Tom, decided that Martin's case was a "hopeless cause" and the family would not pursue paying for an appeal, at least according to the *Asheville Citizen*.[561] According to Black-run news sources, the Moore family, including Martin's brother, continued to search for a way to save him.[562]

The Asheville chapter of the NAACP, composed of "several hundred" Black residents, also decided to fight for Moore's life. Reverend Millard Breeding, the chapter president, said in a statement, "We are not interested in obstructing justice if Moore is guilty, but there are some points of the trial of Moore that are not quite clear to me."[563]

The chapter voted to begin raising funds by popular subscription to aid Martin Moore in his appeal. As the *Pittsburgh Courier* wrote, "The degree of uncertainty about the case and the widespread doubt of the hotel employee's partial or total guilt can be estimated by the fact that a number of justice-loving white people have and are contributing variable sums towards a more thorough investigation. One unnamed white woman has donated first."[564]

The *Asheville Citizen* and *Asheville Times*, which published the most content on the investigation and trial, sometimes reserving entire pages for verbatim transcripts from the court stenographer, made it abundantly clear that though they covered the NAACP's quest to aid Moore—albeit briefly—they were certain not only that Moore was guilty but also that justice had been well served, editorializing in the *Citizen*, "Regardless of the question which was raised as to the manner in which the confession of Martin Moore was originally secured, Judge Phillips has voiced the settled conviction of the community and of those best in position to know when he told the jury that in his judgement they reached the only verdict that was possible."[565]

A *Greensboro Daily News* editorial reacted to the verdict differently, "very forcibly [giving] expression to the opinion of many North Carolinians… [that] the conduct of an officialdom which throws any- and everybody into jail, where they are held indefinitely, incommunicado and without a specific charge, invites by that very act careful scrutiny of every detail of the record of which it is a part."[566]

In the wake of the trial's conclusion, newspaper coverage of the Clevenger murder declined rapidly. Even when, at the end of August, a local man shot and killed a cab driver after a verbal altercation over Moore's guilt or innocence, the story and subsequent trial (the shooter was sentenced to twenty-five years in prison for second-degree murder) were given only minimal coverage. The *Asheville Citizen* did not mention which of the men believed Moore was innocent.[567]

NOW AT THE STATE prison, Martin Moore, clothed in gray prison garb and locked in a cell eight steps from the gas chamber door, had all but given up hope. "I might as well tell that I killed her," the jailer reported Moore saying. "Yeah, I might as well tell 'cause they've got me and I am going to die.…No I don't guess there is much they can do for me now. I guess I will just have to die."

"I read in the papers that the gas kind of chokes you but makes you go off to sleep," Moore said, sitting hunched in his cell, apparently relieved that he would not die in the electric chair. "Is that right, mister?" Martin asked a reporter.[568]

"Are you afraid to die, Martin?" was all he received in reply.

PRISONER: Martin Moore

INTERVIEWED BY: Mr. Edwin Gill

CONFESSION OF MARTIN MOORE

Q. Where was the party?

A. Fannie May Gilliam

Q. How long had you been at the party when you left?

A. Around 45 minutes.

Q. Did you drink anything there?

A. They had punch but I didn't drink any.

Q. What time did you leave?

A. 9:15 or 9:00.

Q. Did you go straight to the hotel?

A. I didn't stop.

Q. Did you have the pistol in your pocket then?

A. I had it with me.

Q. Where did you have it?

A. In my pants.

Q. What was the first floor you went to?

A. Second floor.

Q. How many rooms did you go to and try before you went to hers?

A. Two, I believe.

Q. Then you went to her room?

A. Yes, sir.

The first page of Martin Moore's confession to Commissioner of Paroles Edwin Gill, August 26, 1936. *Laurence Brown Collection, Swannanoa Valley Museum & History Center, Black Mountain, North Carolina.*

"No suh, are you? Be here October 1 and I'll have a story for you," Moore told him, not letting on what story he would tell on the eve of his scheduled execution.[569] But it was widely believed among those following the case that Moore—as well as a number of other people associated with the hotel—knew more about the murder than what was presented at trial.[570]

Days later, Edwin Gill, commissioner of paroles at the state prison in Raleigh, at the request of Solicitor Zeb Nettles, asked Martin Moore to confess again without a lawyer present.

"On my first visit, he denied his guilt," Gill told reporters. "On my second visit, Tuesday night, he made a brief confession. On my third visit this afternoon he confirmed his previous confession in great detail." According to Gill, Moore was calm and seemed "resigned to his fate."[571]

The confession was again published in the *Asheville Citizen*, nearly replicating in every detail the story that investigators and the media had been telling since Moore was arrested on August 9.[572] The only section not published directly in the paper was a series of questions Gill asked Moore about his intention to rape Helen.

"Was it fact that you were suffering at the time with a venereal disease?" Gill asked.

Moore gave his typical reply. "Yes, sir."

"And you were sore? Is that right?"

"Yes, sir."

"And that is one of the reasons you had no intention of committing rape?"

"Yes, sir."

"In other words, you contend that one reason you couldn't have gone in to try to rape her was that you were in no condition to rape her because you were suffering from a venereal disease?"

"Yes, sir," Moore agreed again.[573]

MOORE CONTINUED TO ALTERNATELY proclaim his innocence only to then, according to officials, confess again. Despite this, the NAACP reaffirmed their financial support of Moore's appeal.

Sanford Brown filed the appeal and Moore's execution was automatically delayed. Many news outlets decried the stay of execution, calling it "unjust not to go ahead and execute the man." While others felt the opposite. "There has always been a doubt in the minds of many of Moore's guilt in spite of his repeated 'confessions.' There also were several 'confessions' in the Lindbergh kidnap case. We heard no howl for hasty execution of the several people who 'admitted' this terrible crime. Why the howl now for the life of a man whose guilt is questionable in spite of his 'confessions'?"[574]

But when Sanford Brown did not "properly perfect" the appeal (it was filed late and Solicitor Nettles refused to sign it) and, in fact, did not show up for court to represent Moore "because of illness," the court declined to hear the case.[575]

Sanford Brown made another attempt in mid-November to convince the state supreme court to accept Moore's appeal.[576] In response, the chief justice said that a review of the trial would be merely a "fruitless run-around," and the state rescheduled Moore's execution for two weeks later—December 11, 1936.[577]

Martin's only hope now was clemency from North Carolina's governor, John Ehringhaus.[578]

With support from the "white and Negro citizens of Asheville," Reverend Breeding, Asheville's NAACP president, and two other ministers met with commissioner of paroles Edwin Gill, who would make a recommendation to the governor, pleading for him to give them "just a little time" to investigate new evidence in the case.[579]

"We have been praying," Reverend Breeding told Gill, "the churches and the congregations have been praying and agonizing over this boy's fate."[580]

"We believe he is entirely innocent," Breeding said. He told Gill that they were sure the crime was being "pinned on" Moore and that they suspected another man, who they declined to name, of the crime. They did intimate, however, that this man had not previously been linked to the slaying. Breeding also cited recent "blunders" by Buncombe County officials in which two other men were almost wrongly executed.[581]

After hearing their case, Gill merely replied, "What can I do for a man who confesses every phase of the crime?" As he ushered the men out of his office, he promised that he would think it over before telephoning the governor with his recommendation.[582]

WITH ALMOST ALL HOPE extinguished but media interest reignited, journalist John A. Parris Jr. was allowed to make the trip "one flight up the steel stairs to the row of 'living dead' and three cells down the corridor" to interview Martin Moore on death row. Peering through the bars, Parris found Moore hunched over a plate of cold food. It was hot and stuffy. Parris poked his hand into the cell and offered the young man a cigarette. Moore stood and pocketed the smoke.

Moore and Parris were not alone. A Baptist minister, undeterred by the arrival of the reporter, continued preaching a sermon, which now had hit the hour mark. According to Parris, Moore "listened to every word."[583]

Returning to the bench in his cell, Moore sat and took a sip of coffee. "If I had it all to go over with, I'd do a lot different," he told Parris. "I ain't asking much now. There ain't much to ask. I ain't doing nothing much but reading the Bible. It's the only book I want to read."[584]

Moore seemed to know it was unlikely his life would be spared by the state. "I want to be baptized, that's all. I ain't afraid to die. I hope I go to heaven. I want to meet my mother there. Death can't be so bad. Won't you get 'em to baptize me?"[585]

The next day, more journalists were allowed in to see Moore. "I'm all right with God now, all my sins are forgiven, and I think I'm going to heaven," Moore told them, adding, "I've written to my brother to come and get my body Friday morning." Several asked about the trial, but Moore refused to comment. As the reporters turned to leave, Moore added one last thing. "Come back," he said. "I'll have a whole lot to say later in the week."[586]

Two days before Moore's scheduled execution, two local ministers came to the jail at Moore's request. Dressed in his underwear and a pair of prison pants, Moore kneeled in a small bathtub and lowered himself backward into the water. He rose from the tub silently, now baptized into the Christian faith.[587]

While Moore dried himself, a phone in the warden's office rang; the governor would not intervene on Moore's behalf.[588]

Back in his cell in a dry prison uniform, Moore sat on his cot and picked up a prayer book. When he learned of the governor's decision, he said to one of his visitors, a man from the Department of Public Welfare, "If Roddy would only tell the truth....It just goes to show you can't rely on a friend."[589]

A FEW DAYS EARLIER, Sheriff Brown had opened a letter from the warden at Central Prison, pulling out five tickets to Moore's execution. The warden explained, "The law allows only six tickets for each Execution, and I am sending you all the Law allows except one, as I feel your County is entitled to them more than any one else. Am holding one for a special friend that I have here, that I want to accomodate [sic]. Please...don't issue any to minors or women. In case you do not care to use all these tickets, will ask that you wire me not later than Thursday Noon, as I have a big demand for tickets for this particular Execution."[590]

The warden told reporters, "I guess I've turned away 2,000 persons, not only from this State but from Virginia, Georgia, and South Carolina. It's been phone calls, phone calls, phone calls—letters, letters, letters—for the

STATE OF NORTH CAROLINA
## STATE HIGHWAY AND PUBLIC WORKS COMMISSION
CAPUS M. WAYNICK, CHAIRMAN

JAMES A. HARDISON
E. F. ALLEN
FRANK W. MILLER

ROSS M. SIGMON
JULIEN WOOD
W. C. WOODARD

RALEIGH, N. C.      December 7, 1936

Sheriff Lawrence Brown
Sheriff Buncomb County,
Asheville, N.C.

Dear Sheriff:-          RE: Martin Moore.

I am encloseing herewith five tickets for the execution
of the above named, which will take place Friday December
11th, at 10-30 A.M..The law allows only six tickets for
each Execution, and I am sending you all the Law allows
except one, as I feel your County is entitled to them more
than any oneelse. Am holding one for a special friend that
I have here, that I want to accomodate. Please insert the
names of the one you issue these tickets too in the blank
space, and don,t issue any to minors or women. In case
you do not care to use all these tickets, will ask that
you wire me not later than Thursday Noon, as I have a big
demand for tickets for this particular Execution.

With kindest personal regards,I am

Yours very truly

H.H.Honeycutt
Warden

Letter from the warden at Central Prison in Raleigh, North Carolina, to Sheriff Laurence Brown, December 7, 1936. *Laurence Brown Collection, Swannanoa Valley Museum & History Center, Black Mountain, North Carolina.*

last 10 days." There was no indication of who would receive the sixth ticket. Helen's uncle William told reporters, "I don't say I'll be there, and I don't say I won't be there."[591]

That evening, shortly after Moore's last meal was served, several other prisoners in nearby cells sang a hymn. Moore did not join in and made no last requests, even declining a pack of cigarettes. Instead, he continued to talk to the reporters stationed outside his door. He sighed. "I don't know whether my brother Tom will get here tomorrow for my body or not. Tonight's his night off."[592] Along with a letter, Martin had left Tom a religious booklet, a story and two rings.[593]


MARTIN MOORE AWOKE THE next morning in his unheated cell, heavy rain leaking through the roof. He was soon joined by two ministers who sat and prayed with him as the hour of his execution approached. He told them, along with the warden, that the state was set to "kill an innocent man."[594]

Just after 10:30 a.m., the warden led Martin and the clergymen from the cell to walk the thirteen steps to the execution chamber.[595] Entering the small white room, Moore said, "I'm going to live—for God."[596]

Wearing only a pair of white shorts, Martin, now trembling, tears running down his cheeks, sat in the straight-backed oak chair. The guards wrapped leather straps around his arms and taped a long-range stethoscope over his heart.[597]

"Have you anything to say, Martin?" the warden asked.

Moore looked up at him, his eyes half closed. The warden repeated the question.

"No, sir," Moore replied.[598]

The guards cleared the room and sealed the airtight door.

Law enforcement officers and reporters were the only other faces staring back at Moore through the chamber's large "double-thick" glass window. His family was not allowed to see him. No one from Helen's family attended. Only one of the officers assigned to the case, Love Gudger, had made the trip to Raleigh.[599]

"All right," the warden whispered.

As the executioner tripped a lever on the control board and the lights changed from red to green, the ministers sang, "Pass me not, O Gentle Saviour, Pass me not." Moore quietly joined in, his voice breaking.

Sixteen cyanide pellets fell into a pan filled with sulfuric acid beneath Martin's chair. Fumes rose, creating a thick fog, circulated by fans and filling the room. For the first three minutes, Martin held his breath, refusing to inhale the bluish cloud "floating around his head like cigarette smoke." Martin gasped, needing oxygen. He gave up, took three deep breaths, as he had been instructed to do to speed the process, and his head fell back against the chair.[600]

*Left*: Martin Moore, August 1936. *E.M. Ball Photographic Collection, D.H. Ramsey Library Special Collections, UNC–Asheville, 28804.*

*Below*: Martin Moore's death certificate, December 11, 1936. *North Carolina Bureau of Vital Statistics.*

## STANDARD CERTIFICATE OF DEATH

BUREAU OF VITAL STATISTICS

1. PLACE OF DEATH

County **Wake** — Registration District No. **92-90** — Certificate No. **894**

Township **Raleigh** — or Village

City **Raleigh** — No. **835 W. Morgan St Central Prison** — St.

Length of residence in city or town where death occurred yrs. **3** mos. **13** ds. How long in U.S. if of foreign birth? yrs. mos. ds.

2. FULL NAME **Martin Moore**

(a) Residence: No. **835 W. Morgan** St. Ward. **Raleigh**

PERSONAL AND STATISTICAL PARTICULARS

3. SEX **M**

4. COLOR OR RACE **Colored**

5. Single, Married, Widowed, or Divorced **Single**

5a. If married, widowed, or divorced — HUSBAND of (or) WIFE of

6. DATE OF BIRTH (month, day, and year) **5-15-1914**

7. AGE Years **22** Months **5** Days **11**

8. Trade, profession, or particular kind of work done, as spinner, sawyer, bookkeeper, etc. **Hotel**

9. Industry or business in which work was done, as silk mill, saw mill, bank, etc.

10. Date deceased last worked at this occupation (month and year)

11. Total time (years) spent in this occupation

12. BIRTHPLACE (city or town) **Pauline** (State or country) **South Carolina**

13. NAME **John Moore**

14. BIRTHPLACE (city or town) **Pauline** (State or country) **South Carolina**

15. MAIDEN NAME **Celia Wilson**

16. BIRTHPLACE (city or town) **Pauline** (State or country) **South Carolina**

17. INFORMANT **Celia Moore** (Address) **84½ Hill St, Asheville NC**

18. BURIAL, CREMATION, OR REMOVAL Place **Wake Forest College** **12-12-1936**

19. UNDERTAKER **Brown's Funeral Home** (Address) **Raleigh**

20. FILED **12-14-1936** **W.C. Bulla**

MEDICAL CERTIFICATE OF DEATH

21. DATE OF DEATH (month, day, and year) **Dec. 11, 1936**

22. I HEREBY CERTIFY, That I attended deceased from **Aug. 24, 1936,** to **Dec. 11, 1936**

I last saw h alive on **Dec. 11, 1936** death is said to have occurred on the date stated above, at **10:30 a.m.**

The principal cause of death and related causes of importance in order of onset were as follows:

**Asphyxiation Pursuant to Court order of Buncombe County Superior Court.**

Contributory causes of importance not related to principal cause:

Name of operation — date of

What test confirmed diagnosis? — Was there an autopsy?

23. If death was due to external causes (violence) fill in also the following:

Accident, suicide, or homicide? — Date of injury 19

Where did injury occur?

Specify whether injury occurred in industry, in home, or in public place.

Manner of injury

Nature of injury

24. Was disease or injury in any way related to occupation of deceased?

If so, specify

(Signed) **Yes** M.D.

(Address) **Raleigh NC**

"It was probably the first time a newspaper man ever listened to a dying man's heart as his life was taken from him," wrote reporter John A. Parris Jr., who sat in the control chamber with a long-range stethoscope pressed to his ear.[601]

"His heart sounded like a tom-tom in the stethoscope as the lethal gas was liberated. It went boom, boom, boom." Parris jotted notes as he watched Moore's final moments. Martin's body began to "twist and jerk." Less than a minute later, he lost consciousness and his chin slumped to his chest.

"Six minutes later, the body was hanging limp in the heavy leather straps that propped it up in the big chair, but the pulse beat was 104," Parris wrote. "My notes show that after the seventh minute the body took a mighty lunge, and then at eight minutes after the deadly fumes of gas had been unloosed it was stilled again."

Behind the glass partition, Martin's heart beat began to slow down. The prison physician whispered to the journalist, "The heart is growing weaker. Moore will be dead in another minute. Watch his body for 30 seconds."

And then it was over. Parris noted, "There was a patter of rain on the roof, but no sound of the heart beat, and after a pause the physician signaled to turn on the air pumps and blow the fumes from the chamber."[602]

## 12

# READ THIS IF YOU THINK HE WAS!

The day after Martin's death, well-known professor, author and orator William Pickens sat down at his desk and wrote an article for the Associated Negro Press. Over the next two weeks, the article was published in Black-run newspapers across the country under a number of different titles, including, "Was Martin Moore Guilty of Hotel Murder? Read This If You Think He Was!" "God! What a World!" and "Pickens Tells 'Inside Story' of Co-Ed 'Slayer' Death."[603]

Pickens began by questioning Erwin Pittman's eyewitness account. "A white man," Pickens wrote, "saw a man standing in the girl's room door.… If this person had been a six foot black, that guest would have noticed it. But he described him as another white—never even hinted that he could have been black.…And how the whites do work together in such an emergency. [Pittman] aided the black-hunt now by changing his testimony, saying he was not just sure that the intruder whom he saw said: 'That's what I was wondering,' but maybe he had said: 'Dat's Whut I'se wunderin.'"[604]

Pickens picked apart the investigation, confession and trial, condemning Sheriff Brown's urgency to solve the case as the election approached as well as Martin's forced confession and the "mere formality" of his defense—many of the same complaints already voiced by other journalists and members of the general public.

But about midway through the article, Pickens released a bombshell, a tidbit of information that had so far not been put in print. Pickens wrote:

*And now some sidelights that courts never hear, and would not consider if they did hear them. While the hunt for the slayer was going on, the telephone rang in the home of one of the "biggest" white men in Asheville. He was in his bath, and his wife was out, so that the colored maid had to answer the phone. The caller was another well-known white man and hearing that the other man could not come to the phone and in the excitement mistaking the voice for that of the madam of the house said: "Well, you tell him that we have found out who killed that Clevenger girl: it was the degenerate son of.........."*

*The maid, with fear and confusion, exclaimed, "Wait, I can't tell him that—I'll call him and you'll have to tell him yourself." When the bather heard who it was, he brought his wet body to the phone and after asked the maid: "How much did you hear?" She told him. "Well," said he, "just forget you heard anything."*

*The degenerate son named as the killer is a well-known pervert who lived in the hotel where the killing occurred....But the degenerate was got out of town the next morning, so that he was never questioned. He had been in trouble before.*[605]

Was this the same rumor that had been circulating early on in the investigation? The rumor that William Clevenger referred to on his release from custody; the rumor the *Asheville Citizen* alluded to in a paragraph tacked on to the end of a July 27 article, which mentioned "the son of a prominent Asheville businessman" as being arrested in connection with the murder—a rumor that was quickly and publically "spiked" without the name of the son or his father being printed?[606] Or was this another man entirely?

Then, on January 23, 1937, more than a month after Martin Moore died, the *Pittsburgh Courier*, in an article titled "Did Innocent Man Die for Hotel Crime?" reported, "Although the daily papers refuse to divulge the facts, it is known that Sheriff Lawrence [*sic*] Brown has taken Banks Taylor and Robert and L.D. Ro[ddy], brothers...back into custody as part of the further investigation of the murder case....It is known that before Moore was executed, he wrote a letter to one of the Ro[ddy] brothers begging him to tell the truth about the possession of his (Moore's) gun the night the girl was slain....[Moore] strenuously contended he had loaned [the gun] to Ro[ddy] some time before the tragic night. Ro[ddy], it is said, reloaned the revolver to the son of a very prominent white man in the city."[607]

Still, due to libel laws, which at the time could result in criminal—rather than civil—penalties, no newspapers named the prominent father or his son.

But in 1995, a former employee of the Battery Park Hotel, Booker T. Sherrill, brought up Martin Moore unprompted in an oral history interview. Sherrill, when asked about his wedding day, said, "I'll never forget our wedding because we got married on Saturday and the next day, Sunday, August 1936, Martin Moore confessed to murdering that Clevenger girl. Do you remember that?" Sherrill's new wife, Ruby Taylor, was Banks Taylor's sister.

"I thought everyone remembered that Clevenger case," Sherrill continued when the interviewer responded in the negative. "The night of that murder, that was my short day. I was off at 6:30 that night so I wasn't questioned because it happened late that night or early morning….But so many people think that case never was solved….They never did feel that justice had been done. So many people seemed to think that gun had been planted and Martin Moore was just a scape goat," Sherrill explained. "And I don't think he did it for this reason…after the murder he worked there for about a week or more…and to be frank with you I don't think he had the mentality to have done a crime like that."[608] Sherrill felt that Martin had significant intellectual disabilities.[609]

"Of course," Sherrill continued, "at that time I was very low key and I kept my thoughts to myself. I didn't express them. You can't afford to express your thoughts on a situation like that. Not and work here [at the Battery Park Hotel] and do well."

Then, nearly sixty years after Helen died, Sherrill implicated the son of a prominent white man in the murder. "Some of the people connected our manager's son—at the time Pat Branch was our manager—some of them said his son had something to do with it."[610]

In 1936, BRANCH HAD two adult sons, thirty-seven-year-old Gene and twenty-two-year-old Pat Jr. Sherrill did not specify which son was suspected of the crime. The interviewer did not ask further questions.

Pat's eldest son, Eugene "Gene" Rankin Branch, had attended a private boarding high school for boys in Virginia. Then, after one semester of studies at the University of Virginia, he returned to Asheville. At the end of 1918, Gene began clerking and living at a hotel owned by his father, Margo Terrace.[611] By then the tall, "husky" young man with gray eyes and brown hair was already "one of the city's best known," at least partially because his maternal grandfather had been the city's mayor.[612] Gene was often featured in the society pages, which chronicled his travels as well as dinner parties he threw at Margo Terrace.[613]

Gene Branch (*far left*) and Pat Branch Jr. (*far right*) with their mother, circa 1940s. *North Carolina Collection, Pack Memorial Public Library, Asheville, North Carolina.*

During the 1920s, Pat Sr. and his wife divorced. Pat Jr., their younger son, stayed with his mother and attended the local public high school. Pat Sr. soon remarried and had two daughters.[614]

In 1925, Gene and his girlfriend, Kaye, eloped.[615] Gene began managing Margo Terrace for its new owner, Edwin W. Grove, who was simultaneously tearing down and rebuilding the Battery Park Hotel next door.[616] Gene quickly became well known for his hotel work and served as secretary-treasurer for the Western North Carolina Hotel Men's Association and the Southern Hotel Association.[617]

But Margo Terrace, located on real estate more valuable than the aging hotel, closed at the end of 1928.[618] Gene and Kaye moved to Winchester, Virginia, so that Gene could manage the George Washington Hotel, a one-hundred-room inn just sixty miles outside of Washington, D.C.[619] After

Pat Branch Sr. and Gene Branch in an editorial cartoon. Asheville Citizen, *February 1, 1926.*

less than five years in Virginia, on August 13, 1933, Kaye passed away. Her obituary listed pneumonia as her cause of death,[620] but her death certificate told a different story. While the principal cause was "Lobar Pneumonia, both lungs," the contributory cause was listed as "poison dose of Luminal," and suicide was checked and underlined in red.[621]

Almost exactly one year before Helen Clevenger was murdered in Asheville, Gene remarried.[622] By all appearances, Gene and his new bride resided happily at the George Washington Hotel in Virginia throughout the summer of 1936.

Pat Jr., though his name appeared far less in the papers than his older brother, did seem to be residing in Asheville that fateful summer. The young, single man had attended the University of North Carolina at Chapel Hill beginning in 1931 before returning to the city of his birth in 1933 without a degree. At some point before June 1937, he found work with the Gate City Life Insurance Company in Asheville.[623]

In newspaper coverage of the investigation and trial, including verbatim transcripts recorded by the court stenographer, there is no mention of either of Branch's sons. But tucked in a box of papers donated by Sheriff Brown's family to the museum in his hometown of Black Mountain, North Carolina, between a selection of photographs, telegrams, and news articles related to his investigation into Helen's murder, is a carbon copy of a letter to the chief of police of Winchester, Virginia. The letter, written by Sheriff Brown on July 30, 1936, reads: "I would like a confidential investigation of Mr. Eugene Branch who is, or has been, an assistant manager of a hotel in your city. I would like to know of his deportment and conduct and reputation while in Winchester and whether he has a reputation there for

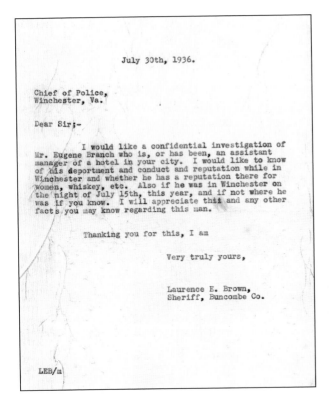

July 30th, 1936.

Chief of Police,
Winchester, Va.

Dear Sir:-

I would like a confidential investigation of Mr. Eugene Branch who is, or has been, an assistant manager of a hotel in your city. I would like to know of his deportment and conduct and reputation while in Winchester and whether he has a reputation there for women, whiskey, etc. Also if he was in Winchester on the night of July 15th, this year, and if not where he was if you know. I will appreciate this and any other facts you may know regarding this man.

Thanking you for this, I am

Very truly yours,

Laurence E. Brown,
Sheriff, Buncombe Co.

LEB/m

Letter from Sheriff Brown to Winchester, Virginia chief of police, July 30, 1936. *Laurence Brown Collection, Swannanoa Valley Museum & History Center, Black Mountain, North Carolina.*

women, whiskey, etc. Also if he was in Winchester on the night of July 15th, this year, and if not where he was if you know. I will appreciate this and any other facts you may know regarding this man."[624]

There is no record of whether Brown received a reply to his inquiry or why he was interested in Gene. It was, however, the only item in the collection of materials that asked for investigation into a specific individual whose name was not mentioned in newspaper reports. Less than a week after Brown sent the letter, a week in which law enforcement grew suddenly silent and released little information to the press, the investigation shifted to look exclusively at Black men.[625]

A LITTLE OVER A month after Martin Moore's execution, still another inquiry into Helen's murder began. In October 1936, the Clevenger family filed a $50,000 lawsuit against the owners of the Battery Park Hotel and manager Pat Branch, alleging "gross negligence," which resulted in Helen's death.[626] The hotel and its insurance company refused to pay the family on the

As the Story Was Reconstructed, Lightning Must Have Revealed to the Girl the Form of the Tall Negro Boy in the Room. She Screamed. He Attacked Her With a Knife and a Pistol.

This graphic, incorrectly putting a knife in Helen's killer's hands, was published in the *San Francisco Examiner* a month after Martin Moore's death, January 10, 1937. The article it accompanied discussed whether a hotel should be held liable for the murder of a guest.

grounds that "an innocent man ha[d] been executed." They planned to begin their own investigation.[627]

More than a year after the lawsuit was filed, however, due a technicality—the Clevengers had listed the Knott Management Corporation instead of the Knott Hotel Company as the defendant—the suit was settled out of court for $6,000. The Helen Clevenger murder case was officially closed.[628]

# 13

# EPILOGUE

Though the intense media interest in Helen's murder died with Moore at the end of 1936, most of those associated with the investigation felt the aftereffects of the deaths of the two young people for years. Battery Park Hotel bell captain Booker T. Sherrill remembered, "That was quite a trying time around here. Race relations during that time. Just on edge....[The Clevenger case] upset this city and it took 8, 9, 10 years for the people to relax."[629]

Joe Ury, the first person detained by law enforcement in connection with Helen's murder, moved with his wife and son to Houston, Texas, in the late 1930s to work on the railroad. He died in Houston in 1991.[630]

Mark Wollner continued his career as a violinist before winning acclaim as a painter later in life. In 1961, he married Mary Brooks, a concert pianist, who had also been his accompanist in 1936. The couple continued to travel but spent at least part of their time at their home in Hendersonville, North Carolina, just outside of Asheville.[631] Wollner's alibi witness, Mildred Ward, married and moved to Washington, D.C.[632]

Night watchman Daniel Gaddy and his wife, Sue, had two more sons. The family continued to reside in Asheville, where Gaddy spent the rest of his career managing the Battery Park parking lot. He died unexpectedly of a heart attack in 1970 at the age of sixty-two.[633]

Banks Taylor moved to Mount Vernon, New York, shortly after the trial. He died in 1970 at age fifty-eight after a long illness.[634]

L.D. Roddy and his wife eventually moved to Baltimore, Maryland, where he died in 1963 at fifty-four years old. His body was returned to Asheville for burial.[635]

William L. Clevenger continued to teach at North Carolina State College until he died in his sleep at age sixty-nine while representing the college at the annual meeting of the American Dairy Science Association in Knoxville, Tennessee. The previous March, the college had created an endowment for a W.L. Clevenger Research Fellowship in Dairy Manufacturing. Helen's murder claimed the third paragraph in his death announcement.[636]

HELEN'S PARENTS, JOSEPH AND Mary Clevenger, stayed in Staten Island until Mary's death in 1943. Mary was buried beside her three children in Fletcher, Ohio; their deaths were detailed in her obituary. Joseph remarried and continued working for the Food and Drug Administration in New York until retiring in 1944. He died unexpectedly the following year while he and his second wife were visiting friends in Washington, D.C. He was buried with Mary and his children in Fletcher, Ohio.[637]

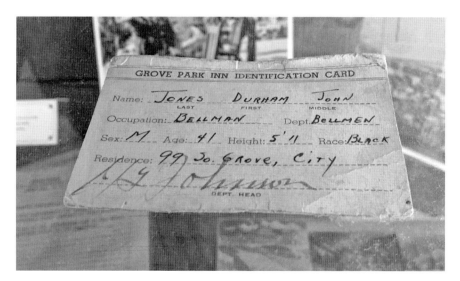

Durham Jones, witness and former Battery Park Hotel employee, identification card, Grove Park Inn, 1942, on display at the Grove Park Inn, 2021. On the back of the card is Jones's right index fingerprint. In the wake of Helen's murder, there was a push to keep employee fingerprints on file in case of a crime. *Photograph by author.*

WALTER B. ORR, THE former chief of police from Charlotte, North Carolina, insisted that he deserved the $1,000 reward for the capture and conviction of Martin Moore. In explanation, Orr told reporters, "I threatened Banks Taylor I would charge him with the crime and held him four days before he told me what I wanted to know [about Martin Moore owning a pistol]." Orr bragged that "before he even left Charlotte" he knew "he would arrest one…of the negro employees"[638] and that the detectives from New York played a "negligible" role in the investigation.[639]

The elder of the New York detectives, Thomas J. Martin, was quick to respond to Orr's slight. "I don't know what Orr did in this case. He did nothing while I was there. All I can say is that the crime was there 12 days before we got there and was solved two days after we arrived. Now dope it out for yourself." Because he solved the case in the line of duty, Thomas Martin said, he was ineligible to receive the reward, but if not for the restrictions, he believed that the reward should be divided between the "three men in the sheriff's office who worked hard and capably on the case, and [Detective John J.] Quinn and myself."[640]

Ultimately, Orr was the only person to claim part of the reward. He died in 1957 at seventy-four years old.[641]

In 1939, Detective Quinn died of uremic poisoning at age thirty-one.[642] Detective Martin retired from the New York Police Department as acting sergeant in July 1945 after thirty-seven years of service. He died less than five months later at the age of sixty-four.[643] Both of their death announcements mentioned their role in Martin Moore's arrest.[644]

Solicitor Zebulon Vance Nettles was elected as a superior court judge in 1938, a position he held until his retirement. He died in 1976 at eighty-two years of age. His obituary read, in part, "As Superior Court solicitor, he prosecuted many memorable cases in Buncombe county, including…the trial of Martin Moore, who was executed in 1936 for the murder of Helen Clevenger at the Battery Park Hotel."[645]

J. Scroop Styles, one of Martin Moore's court-appointed lawyers, died in 1967. His obituary noted, "Known to never flinch from the challenge of a hard criminal case, some bordering on the impossible, Mr. Styles saved a total of 193 defendants charged with capital crimes from execution by the state. All of the juries which found his clients guilty recommended mercy, which is automatically a life sentence in this state." The obituary also mentioned Martin Moore by name. It read, "Styles was one of two court-appointed defense lawyers for Martin Moore…[who] were relieved from the case by the judge before the sentence was passed."[646]

Sheriff Laurence E. Brown won reelection in 1936 and again in every election for the next quarter century until a surprise defeat in 1962. Lewis Green, an *Asheville Citizen-Times* reporter, staunch Republican and unapologetic bigot, who made a name for himself—and plenty of enemies—with his muckraking journalism, wrote of Brown's electoral loss in his 2003 memoir:

> *He had it so close. Brown lost by 146 votes, then called for a recount. I went to the basement of the Courthouse, where Brown had retained some lawyers. One was a young lawyer, who went behind the curtains of a couple of machines, came out to confer with colleagues a moment, then said: "We don't want a recount." People in the know told me later that* [his opponent] *had won by a couple of thousand of votes. The Democrats stole all they could and still lost. They did not take it in stride. On the day* [the new sheriff] *was sworn in, he found cruiser battery and radio cables cut, uniforms piled up and pissed on by outgoing deputies, anti-freeze drained. I made photos. They allowed me to print nothing at C-T* [Asheville Citizen-Times]."[647]

The editor of the Asheville paper allegedly told Green, "Lewis, the chief deputy is my brother. Family gets in the way of principle."[648]

By the time of the 1962 election, Laurence and his brother, former deputy Tom K. Brown, who had been accused of beating Martin Moore, had fallen out. Tom supported his brother's opponent and, on election day, got into a drunken brawl with Laurence's right-hand-man, Deputy Jake Robertson. According to Robertson, "I was outside [the polling place]…and we had a few words.…And before I could bat my eye [Tom] whupped me upside the head.…I knew he kept a gun in his right front pocket. Had a little snub-nosed .28 hammerless…so that was my thought right quick. I had to get that.…I was having trouble getting him on the ground so I kicked his right leg out from under him and when I did it broke his ankle.

"And of course after I got his gun," Robertson continued, I called [Sheriff Brown] and told the sheriff that he was out there and he" was intoxicated and he said, 'Jake, I'll be out there as quick as I can get there.' And he told Tom, 'You get off these grounds. You're going to do it right now or I'm a take you over there and put you in jail and keep you there as long as I feel I ought to.'"[649]

Laurence Brown died of cancer in 1965, just three years after losing the election. The front-page article in the *Asheville Times* noted, "Laurence

Brown's ability to track down a criminal—no matter how scarce the clues—has become almost legendary. Perhaps the most famous case was the murder during the thirties of 19-year-old Helen Irene Clevenger, student and socialite."[650] After Laurence's death, Tom unsuccessfully ran for Buncombe County sheriff twice.[651]

Though the Brown family who lived into the twenty-first century still celebrated Laurence Brown's role in Martin Moore's conviction, they knew few details about the case. However, one of the sheriff's grandsons remembered, "There was some story that [Martin Moore] was beaten into confession. Of course those were all things that were put down by the Republicans. I know there was a lot of that that went back and forth trying to shoot [the sheriff] down…[but] it's like any law enforcement department, you're going to have a couple deputies that shouldn't be there."[652]

MANAGER BRANCH RETIRED TWO years after Helen's murder and died in Asheville in 1961, leaving behind his four children.[653] His youngest son, Pat Branch Jr., married less than a year after Helen's murder and resided in Asheville until 1940, when he became assistant manager of the Burlington, North Carolina branch of Gate City Life Insurance Company. His older brother, Gene, continued to manage the George Washington Hotel in Winchester, Virginia, until his retirement. Both men married three times. Gene died of a heart attack in 1980. Pat Jr. died in 2000.[654]

MARTIN'S MOTHER, CELIE, VACATED 84½ Hill Street, where deputies had taken her youngest son into custody, and moved in with another son, Tom, and his family a few houses down the street. She continued to reside on Hill Street until at least 1951 and likely died soon thereafter.[655] By the end of the decade, most of the homes lining Hill Street were demolished to make way for a new Crosstown Expressway, the first victims of an urban renewal process that for the next thirty years would systematically dismantle many of Asheville's historically Black communities.

The Battery Park Hotel closed in 1972, and the abandoned building suffered from neglect. But after being added to the National Register of Historic Places in 1979, the hotel was renovated and converted to senior living apartments. Booker T. Sherrill, another victim of the Hill Street demolitions, who had never been allowed to enter through the hotel's front door during his nearly forty-year career as bell captain, moved into an

Battery Park Hotel lobby, 1977. *National Register, Division of Archive & History, Raleigh, North Carolina.*

apartment on the fourth floor. In a 1985 story in the *Citizen-Times*, Sherrill said, "Living in the Battery Park today is a grand and glorious feeling."[656]

LESS THAN A WEEK after Martin's execution, when no one arrived at the undertaker to claim his body, Wake Forest Medical School in Raleigh procured his cadaver without his or his family's consent through the State Anatomical Commission. The medical school paid only the cost of "embalming services and delivery,"[657] a cost that Martin's family could likely not afford, even to fulfill his last request.

The *Wake Forest Alumni News* published a short piece alongside tidbits about new band uniforms and glee club performances, announcing the medical school's new acquisition, which read, in part:

> *Martin Moore, gangling negro recently executed for murdering Helen Clevenger, may have been North Carolina's No. 1 criminal, but to Wake Forest college medical students his body, which arrived here this week from Raleigh, is just corpse No. 96. His tall frame had to be placed diagonally in the tin-lined box filled with a solution where he will repose until medical students start carving on him next September. A 100-lb. iron weight holds*

*Moore under the surface along with three of his fellow countrymen, all awaiting dissection day. Except for a grey pallor and closed eyes, Moore looks much as he did before he walked to his death in the Raleigh gas chamber.*[658]

What happened to Martin Moore's body after being dissected is currently unknown. If unclaimed by his family—and most cadavers remained unclaimed simply due to the cost of claiming them—Martin should have been laid to rest inside a pine box in an unmarked grave in the segregated Wake Forest Cemetery.[659]

But in 1966, a construction worker digging a foundation near the former location of the medical school (which had moved to Winston-Salem, North Carolina in 1940) stumbled upon human "leg bones, arm bones...but no skulls" scattered among "old tin cans and other trash." The bones—enough to "put together three or four men"—were loaded in the county coroner's trunk for further analysis. Dr. George Mackie, who had attended the medical school in the 1920s and returned as a professor in 1930, told the coroner, "It [is] possible medical students buried the bones in the trash pit after the cadavers had been dissected."

"What happened to the skulls?" the coroner asked.

Dr. Mackie responded, "I understand medical students used to make ash trays out of the skulls."[660]

# NOTES

## Chapter 1

1. "Father Had Dream His Daughter Faced Peril," *Asheville Citizen*, July 23, 1936.
2. "Clevenger Is Highly Regarded as Teacher, Aver His Associates," *Asheville Citizen*, July 24, 1936.
3. Ibid.
4. "Mother Is Dazed by Fate of Her Daughter," *Asheville Citizen*, July 18, 1936; " Mother Urged Helen Not to Attempt Trip," *Morning Post* (Camden, NJ), July 21, 1936.
5. "Expect Grand Jury to Get Moore Case Today," *Asheville Citizen*, August 20, 1936.
6. "Miss Clevenger Wrote Parents About Her Trip," *Asheville Citizen*, July 30, 1936; "Girl's Letter Shows She Was in Happy Mood," *Asheville Times*, July 30, 1936.
7. "Arrest Made in Clevenger Murder Case," *Asheville Citizen*, July 18, 1936.
8. Suzanna Smith Miles, "Queen of the Hill: Grand and Posh, the Original Battery Park Hotel Ushered in Asheville's Tourism Boom," *WNC Magazine*, May 2010.
9. Thomas Calder, "Asheville Archives: Flames Finish Off the Original Battery Park Hotel, 1923," *Mountain XPress*, October 9, 2018; "Battery Park Hotel," National Register of Historic Places, 1977.

10. Rob Neufeld, "Visiting Our Past: Old Battery Park Hotel Yielded to New in 1922," *Asheville Citizen-Times*, August 6, 2017.

11. Ibid.

12. "Battery Park Hotel," National Register of Historic Places.

13. Thomas Wolfe, *You Can't Go Home Again* (New York: Harper & Row, 1940).

14. Miles, "Queen of the Hill"; Cate Huguelet, "Writer's Retreats: Author F. Scott Fitzgerald's Frequent Visits to the Mountains Yielded a Turning Point Amid Dark Days," *WNC Magazine*, May 2013.

15. "Battery Park Hotel," National Register of Historic Places.

16. Ibid.

17. Booker T. Sherrill, Oral History, February 27, 1995, UNCA Special Collections.

18. "Battery Park Hotel," National Register of Historic Places.

19. Ibid.

20. Ibid.

21. "Miss Clevenger Wrote Parents."

22. "Murdered Girl Stopped Here Sunday Night," *Cherokee Scout*, July 23, 1936.

23. "Arrest Made in Clevenger Murder."

24. "Three Men Held in Clevenger Case," *Asheville Citizen*, July 19, 1936.

25. "State's Witnesses Link Moore with Slaying," *Asheville Citizen*, August 21, 1936.

26. "Arrest Made in Clevenger Murder."

27. "Find Few Clues in Pretty Girl's Murder at Hotel," *Asheville Citizen*, July 17, 1936.

28. Peter Levins, "When Justice Triumphed," *New York Daily News*, May 3, 1942.

29. Ibid.

30. "Fingerprints in Clevenger Case Studied," *Asheville Citizen*, August 1, 1936.

31. Ibid.

32. "Tells of Screams Heard from Room Night of Slaying," *Asheville Citizen*, July 29, 1936.

33. Ibid.; "State's Witnesses Link Moore"; H.G. Trotter, "Witnesses Tell of Finding Helen's Body," *Charlotte Observer*, August 20, 1936.

34. Love Gudger and Tom K. Brown, as told to Herbert Rudlin, "The Rapist Murder of Co-Ed Clevenger," *Official Detective Stories*, October 15, 1936.

35. Levins, "When Justice Triumphed."

36. Gudger, Brown and Rudlin, "Rapist Murder."

37. "Find Few Clues."
38. "Officers Study Blood Stains in Clevenger Case," *Asheville Citizen*, July 28, 1936; Gudger, Brown and Rudlin, "Rapist Murder"; "Chemist Drafts Clevenger Clue Report to Cops," *Record* (Hackensack, NJ), July 31, 1936.
39. Ibid.
40. "Officers Study Blood Stains."
41. "Few Tangible Clues Left by Girl's Slayer," *Asheville Citizen*, August 2, 1936.
42. "Officers Study Blood Stains."
43. "Wollner's Alibi Witness Held for Questioning," *Asheville Citizen*, July 20, 1936.
44. "State's Witnesses Link Moore."
45. "Arrest Made in Clevenger Murder."
46. "Tells of Screams Heard."
47. "N.Y. Experts Link Moore's Gun to Murder," *Charlotte Observer*, August 21, 1936.
48. "Arrest Made in Clevenger Murder"; "Wollner's Alibi Witness Held"; "Few Tangible Clues Left"; Laurence E. Brown, as told to C.R. Sumner, "Revelations of Mystery and Horror in the Helen Clevenger Case," *True Detective Mysteries and Famous Detective Cases*, November 1936.
49. Brown and Sumner, "Revelations of Mystery and Horror."
50. "Few Tangible Clues Left."
51. "Mystery of Girl's Murder Deepens," *Asheville Citizen*, July 26, 1936.
52. "Girl's Uncle Questioned in Slaying," *Asheville Times*, July 25, 1936.
53. Martha Strayer, "The Clevenger Murder," *Knoxville News-Sentinel*, August 2, 1936.
54. "Mystery of Girl's Murder Deepens."
55. Strayer, "Clevenger Murder."
56. Ibid.
57. "Jones Gives Detailed Version of Seeing Man Flee from Hotel Front," *Asheville Citizen*, July 23, 1936.
58. Gudger, Brown and Rudlin, "Rapist Murder."
59. "Jones Gives Detailed Version."
60. "Bits of News Picked Up in Slaying Probe," *Asheville Citizen*, July 29, 1936.
61. "Three Men Held."
62. Ibid.
63. Strayer, "Clevenger Murder."
64. Ibid.

65. Ibid.; Brown and Sumner, "Revelations of Mystery and Horror."
66. "Three Men Held"; "Famed Doctor to Hold Free Clinic in City," *Asheville Citizen*, February 5, 1935.
67. "Arrest Made in Clevenger Murder."
68. "Tells of Screams Heard."
69. "Father Had Dream."
70. "Telegram from Joseph Clevenger to Sheriff Lawrence Brown," Lawrence Brown Papers, Swannanoa Valley Museum & History Center, July 16, 1936.
71. "Mother Is Dazed."
72. "Clevenger Is Highly Regarded."

## *Chapter 2*

73. "Clevenger Returns for Questioning in Probe," *Asheville Citizen*, July 25, 1936; "State Begins Testimony in Clevenger Case," *Asheville Citizen*, August 20, 1936.
74. Ibid.
75. "Says Officers Were Notified Without Delay," *Asheville Citizen*, July 31, 1936; Brown and Sumner, "Revelations of Mystery and Horror."
76. "Clevenger Returns for Questioning"; "State Begins Testimony."
77. "Clevenger Returns for Questioning"; "State Begins Testimony."
78. "Clevenger Returns for Questioning"; "State Begins Testimony."
79. "Few Tangible Clues Left"; "Arrest Made in Clevenger Murder."
80. "State Begins Testimony."
81. "Few Tangible Clues Left."
82. Brown and Sumner, "Revelations of Mystery and Horror."
83. "State Begins Testimony."
84. Brown and Sumner, "Revelations of Mystery and Horror."
85. "Pat Branch, Hotelman, Is Dead at 88," *Asheville Citizen*, October 13, 1961; "Battery Park to Be Put in Charge of Pat H. Branch," *Asheville Citizen*, May 24, 1928.
86. "Clevenger Returns for Questioning"; "State Begins Testimony."
87. "Says Officers Were Notified."
88. Brown and Sumner, "Revelations of Mystery and Horror."
89. "Clevenger Returns for Questioning"; "State Begins Testimony."
90. "State Begins Testimony."
91. Ibid.

92. "Says Officers Were Notified."

93. Brown and Sumner, "Revelations of Mystery and Horror."

94. Ibid.

95. "'Wild Rumor,' Police Chief Tells Inquirer, Then Goes Fishing," *Asheville Times*, July 17, 1936.

96. "City Police Are Taking No Hand in Murder Case," *Asheville Citizen*, July 17, 1936.

97. "Few Tangible Clues Left"; "Arrest Made in Clevenger Murder."

98. Joyce Justus Parris, "Laurence E. Brown," in *A History of Black Mountain and Its People* (Black Mountain, NC: Black Mountain Centennial Commission, 1992), 292–5; "Laurence E. Brown Dies," *Asheville Times*, December 21, 1965.

99. "In Memory of Carey Clyde Brown," *Asheville Citizen*, November 7, 1923; "Grid Star Killed," *Tuscaloosa News and Times Gazette*, October 9, 1923.

100. Harold Hammond, "Sheriff Out After 32 Years," *Charlotte News*, January 1, 1963.

101. Parris, *History of Black Mountain*, 292–5; "Laurence E. Brown Dies."

102. Jay Walker, "That Reminds Me," *Asheville Citizen*, April 26, 1931.

103. "Postmaster Had Lots of Booze," *Statesville Record and Landmark*, December 23, 1926.

104. "J.W. Neely & Sons Advertisement," *Asheville Citizen*, December 22, 1926.

105. Dix Sarsfield, "Officers Wage Fierce War on Mountain Rum," *Asheville Citizen*, July 24, 1936.

106. Laurence E. Brown, "The Bootleggers Union vs. Laurence E. Brown," *Asheville Citizen*, June 1, 1928.

107. "First Time in 32 Years They Win," *Asheville Citizen*, November 7, 1928.

108. Parris, *History of Black Mountain*, 292–5.

109. Gary Sorrells, "History of the Office of the Sheriff, Buncombe County, NC," Western North Carolina Public Service Department, Buncombe County Sheriff's Website, www.wncps.org.

110. Interview with Jake Robertson, Black Mountain, North Carolina, by Jerry Pope and Bert Brown, March 19, 2003, Oral History Collection, Swannanoa Valley Museum & History Center, Black Mountain, North Carolina.

111. Hammond, "Sheriff Out After 32 Years."

112. Cameron Shipp, "Sheriff's Armor-Plated Automobile Is a Wonder," *Charlotte News*, July 27, 1936.

113. "State's Witnesses Link Moore."

114. Ibid.

115. Ibid.

116. Ibid.

117. Gudger, Brown and Rudlin, "Rapist Murder."

118. Brown and Sumner, "Revelations of Mystery and Horror."

119. "State's Witnesses Link Moore."

120. "Staff Men from Eastern Papers Here on Murder," *Asheville Citizen*, July 19, 1936.

121. "Citizen Reporter Is Threatened by Chief of Detectives Here," *Asheville Citizen*, July 18, 1936.

122. "'Wild Rumor.'"

123. "Mother Is Dazed."

124. "Thinks Gaddy Can Provide Solution to Girl's Murder," *Asheville Citizen*, July 22, 1936.

125. "Mother Is Dazed."

126. "Arrest Made in Clevenger Murder"; "First Arrest in Mystery Case."

127. Gudger, Brown and Rudlin, "Rapist Murder."

128. "Arrest Made in Clevenger Murder"; "First Arrest in Mystery Case."

129. "Arrest Made in Clevenger Murder"; Gudger, Brown and Rudlin, "Rapist Murder."

130. "Wollner's Alibi Witness Held for Questioning," *Asheville Citizen*, July 20, 1936.

131. "Bits of News."

132. William Fowlkes Jr., "Seeing and Saying," *Atlanta Daily World*, July 21, 1936.

133. Ibid.

## *Chapter 3*

134. "Uncle Leaves Asheville Jail; Probe Becalmed," *Tampa Tribune*, July 27, 1936; "Slain Students Pleading Bared," *Idaho Evening Times*, July 28, 1936; Gudger, Brown and Rudlin, "Rapist Murder."

135. "Here's One for You to Dope Out and Win $1,000 Award," *Asheville Citizen*, July 28, 1936.

136. "Arrest Made in Clevenger Murder"; "First Arrest in Mystery Case Made by Police," *Asheville Times*, July 18, 1936.

137. "Says Girls Had No Men Friends While in City," *Asheville Citizen*, July 22, 1936.

138. Ibid.

139. "False Clues Run Down in Clevenger Slaying," *Asheville Citizen*, August 2, 1936.

140. "Says Girls Had No Men Friends."

141. Ibid.

142. "Bits of News."

143. "Wollner Widely Known for His Work in Music," *Asheville Citizen*, July 22, 1936.

144. Cameron Shipp, "The Clevenger Case: News Reporter Finds Asheville's Front Page Murder Mystery Stranger Than Fiction," *Charlotte News*, July 26, 1936.

145. "Hotel Pass Key Sheds Light on Slaying of Girl," *Asheville Citizen*, July 20, 1936; Gudger, Brown and Rudlin, "Rapist Murder."

146. "Wollner's Alibi Witness Held."

147. "Wollner Widely Known."

148. "Police Grill Mark Wollner's Alibi Girl," *Charlotte Observer*, July 20, 1936.

149. "Quiz Musician in Hotel Murder of Girl Student," *Times Union* (Brooklyn, NY), July 19, 1936.

150. Shipp, "Clevenger Case."

151. Gudger, Brown and Rudlin, "Rapist Murder."

152. "Wollner Widely Known"; "Wollner's Alibi Witness Held."

153. "Wollner's Alibi Witness Held."

154. Gudger, Brown and Rudlin, "Rapist Murder."

155. Ibid.

156. Ibid.

157. "Three Men Held."

158. Gudger, Brown and Rudlin, "Rapist Murder."

159. Ibid.

160. "Rites for Captain Norvin C. Ward Set for Today," *Times-News* (Hendersonville, NC), February 11, 1933; "Murder Case Being Heard," *Times-News* (Hendersonville, NC), March 10, 1933.

161. Gudger, Brown and Rudlin, "Rapist Murder."

162. "Three Men Held."

163. Ibid.

164. Ibid.

165. Gudger, Brown and Rudlin, "Rapist Murder."

166. Ibid.

167. "Wollner's Alibi Witness Held."

168. Gudger, Brown and Rudlin, "Rapist Murder."

169. "Wollner's Alibi Witness Held."

170. Ibid.

171. Ibid; "Hotel Pass Key Sheds Light."

172. "Three Men Held."

173. "Wollner's Alibi Witness Held."

174. "Brown Reiterates Plan for Arrest of Slayer Today," *Asheville Citizen*, July 23, 1936.

175. Shipp, "Clevenger Case."

176. Cameron Shipp, "Promise to Jail Killer Tonight Still Stands," *Charlotte News*, July 24, 1936.

177. Ibid.

178. Ibid.

179. Ibid.

180. "Wollner Is Impatient, His Jailor Discloses," *Asheville Citizen*, July 21, 1936.

181. Ibid.; "New Attacks Hammer Alibi as Wollner Stays in Cell," *Morning Post* (Camden, NJ), July 21, 1936.

182. "Hotel Pass Key Sheds Light."

183. Ibid.; "Pass Key Adds Clue in Slaying," *Evening Sun* (Hanover, PA), July 21, 1936.

184. Ibid.

185. "Hotel Pass Key Sheds Light."

186. "Wollner's Alibi Witness Held."

187. Ibid.

188. "Fingerprints in Clevenger Case Studied," *Asheville Citizen*, August 1, 1936.

189. "Reveal Bruises Were Found on Thumb of Girl," *Asheville Citizen*, July 24, 1936.

190. "Wollner Is Impatient."

191. Ibid.

192. "Thinks Gaddy Can Provide Solution."

193. Ibid.

194. Ibid; "Brown Predicts Arrest of Slayer in Clevenger Case Within 48 Hours," *Asheville Citizen*, July 23, 1936.

195. "Wollner Entertains Himself in Jail by Playing Classical Music on Violin," *Asheville Citizen*, July 23, 1936.

196. Ibid.

197. "Flowers Are Taken to Wollner by Boy Pupil," *Asheville Citizen*, July 23, 1936.

198. "Thinks Gaddy Can Provide Solution."

199. Ibid.
200. Gudger, Brown and Rudlin, "Rapist Murder."
201. Ibid.
202. Ibid.
203. "Chief Everett out of City on Clevenger Case," *Asheville Citizen*, August 5, 1936; "Letter from Laurence E. Brown to W.M. Allen," August 4, 1936, Brown Collection, Swannanoa Valley Museum & History Center.
204. "Wollner Given Release Lauds Sheriff Brown," *Asheville Citizen*, July 25, 1936.

## *Chapter 4*

205. "Study Two New Clues in Murder Case," *Asheville Times*, July 28, 1936; Gudger, Brown and Rudlin, "Rapist Murder."
206. Brown and Sumner, "Revelations of Mystery and Horror."
207. "Officers Study Blood Stains."
208. Brown and Sumner, "Revelations of Mystery and Horror."
209. Strayer, "Clevenger Murder."
210. Gudger, Brown and Rudlin, "Rapist Murder."
211. Strayer, "Clevenger Murder"; "Thinks Gaddy Can Provide Solution"; Daniel Gaddy, Buncombe County, North Carolina 1930 U.S. Census, population schedule; Daniel Gaddy, Buncombe County, North Carolina 1940 U.S. Census, population schedule.
212. Strayer, "Clevenger Murder."
213. Gudger, Brown and Rudlin, "Rapist Murder."
214. Brown and Sumner, "Revelations of Mystery and Horror."
215. "Three Men Held."
216. Brown and Sumner, "Revelations of Mystery and Horror"; Gudger, Brown and Rudlin, "Rapist Murder."
217. Gudger, Brown and Rudlin, "Rapist Murder."
218. Brown and Sumner, "Revelations of Mystery and Horror."
219. "Thinks Gaddy Can Provide Solution."
220. Ibid.
221. Brown and Sumner, "Revelations of Mystery and Horror"; "Brown Predicts Arrest of Slayer."
222. Brown and Sumner, "Revelations of Mystery and Horror."
223. Gudger, Brown and Rudlin, "Rapist Murder."
224. Brown and Sumner, "Revelations of Mystery and Horror."

225. Ibid.

226. Ibid; "False Clues Run Down."

227. Brown and Sumner, "Revelations of Mystery and Horror."

228. "Clevenger Murder Case Is Solved with Confession of Negro Youth," *Asheville Citizen*, August 10, 1936; "Two More Held in Clevenger Case," *Charlotte News*, July 21, 1936; "Pass Key Adds Clue in Slaying."

229. Gudger, Brown and Rudlin, "Rapist Murder"; "Speedy Trial Planned for Clevenger Slayer," *Asheville Citizen*, August 11, 1936.

230. Brown and Sumner, "Revelations of Mystery and Horror"; "Hotel Pass Key Sheds Light."

231. Brown and Sumner, "Revelations of Mystery and Horror."

232. "Clevenger Returns for Questioning."

233. "Gaddy, Exonerated of Crime, Cries with Joy," *Asheville Citizen*, August 9, 1936.

234. "Thinks Gaddy Can Provide Solution"; "Brown Predicts Arrest of Slayer"; "Gaddy, Exonerated."

235. "Brown Predicts Arrest of Slayer."

236. "Thinks Gaddy Can Provide Solution."

237. Ibid.

238. "Brown Predicts Arrest of Slayer."

239. "Bits of News Picked Up in Slaying Probe," *Asheville Citizen*, July 25, 1936.

240. "Brown Predicts Arrest of Slayer."

241. Strayer, "Clevenger Murder."

242. "Brown Reiterates Plan for Arrest of Slayer Today," *Asheville Citizen*, July 24, 1936.

243. Ibid.

244. Ibid.

245. Gudger, Brown and Rudlin, "Rapist Murder"; "Gaddy, Exonerated."

246. "Asheville Sheriff Vows to Jail Slayer of Helen Clevenger Before Nightfall," *Herald Statesman* (Yonkers, NY), July 24, 1936.

247. "Description of Slayer Is Furnished," *Bee* (Danville, VA), July 27, 1936.

248. "Daniel Gaddy Is Enigma of Slaying Case," *Asheville Citizen*, July 26, 1936.

249. "Gaddy's Job as Night Watchman Still in Doubt," *Asheville Citizen*, August 9, 1936.

250. "Bits of News Picked Up in Slaying Probe," *Asheville Citizen*, August 1, 1936.

251. "Witnesses Vary in Description of Men at Hotel," *Asheville Citizen*, July 30, 1936.

252. "Tells of Screams Heard."

253. "Chief Everett out of City."

254. "Fingerprints in Clevenger Case Studied"; Brown and Sumner, "Revelations of Mystery and Horror."

## Chapter 5

255. "Clevenger Sees Early Solution of Murder Case," *Asheville Citizen*, July 19, 1936.

256. Associated Press photo, author's collection.

257. "Thinks Gaddy Can Provide Solution."

258. Brown and Sumner, "Revelations of Mystery and Horror."

259. Ibid.

260. "Clevenger Sees Early Solution."

261. "Face of Murder Victim Remains Calm in Death," *Piqua (OH) Daily Call*, July 21, 1936.

262. "Miss Clevenger Was Believer in Unique Religion," *Asheville Citizen*, July 31, 1936.

263. "If You're Murdered in a Hotel, Is the Hotel Responsible?" *San Francisco Examiner*, January 10, 1937.

264. Find a Grave no. 31600163, "Memorial Page for Helen Clevenger (November 4, 1917–July 1936)," Fletcher Cemetery, Fletcher, Miami County, Ohio, https://www.findagrave.com.

265. "Face of Murder Victim."

266. "Rites for Slain Girl Conducted," *Asheville Citizen*, July 22, 1936.

267. "Clevenger Sees Early Solution"; Find a Grave no. 31600163.

268. Ibid.

269. "Brown Predicts Arrest of Slayer."

270. Ibid.

271. "Father Had Dream."

272. Ibid.

273. "Brown Reiterates Plan for Arrest."

274. Brown and Sumner, "Revelations of Mystery and Horror."

275. "Few Tangible Clues Left."

276. Ibid.

277. "Mystery of Girl's Murder Deepens"; "Prof. Clevenger, Slaying Witness, Leaves Jail Here," *Asheville Citizen*, July 27, 1936; Brown and Sumner, "Revelations of Mystery and Horror."

278. Brown and Sumner, "Revelations of Mystery and Horror."
279. Ibid.
280. "Bits of News Picked Up in Slaying Probe," *Asheville Citizen*, July 25, 1936.
281. Ibid.
282. Ibid.
283. "Clevenger Returns for Questioning."
284. "Girl's Uncle Questioned."
285. "Clevenger Returns for Questioning"; "Few Tangible Clues Left."
286. "Bits of News Picked Up in Slaying Probe," *Asheville Citizen*, July 25, 1936.
287. Ibid.
288. "Murder Is Big Theme of Public," *Asheville Citizen*, July 22, 1936.
289. "Bits of News Picked Up in Slaying Probe," *Asheville Citizen*, July 24, 1936.
290. Ibid.
291. "Family Is Not Upset," *Asheville Citizen*, July 25, 1936.
292. Brown and Sumner, "Revelations of Mystery and Horror."
293. "Mystery of Girl's Murder Deepens."
294. Ibid.; "Prejudice," *News and Observer* (Raleigh, NC), July 27, 1936.
295. "Nothing Is Found in Clevenger's Room to Help Solve Mystery," *Asheville Citizen*, July 26, 1936.
296. "Clevenger Is Highly Regarded."
297. Ibid.
298. "Nothing Is Found in Clevenger's Room."
299. Ibid.
300. "Clevenger Is Highly Regarded."
301. "Nothing Is Found in Clevenger's Room."
302. "Clevenger Is Highly Regarded."
303. Brown and Sumner, "Revelations of Mystery and Horror."
304. "Prof. Clevenger, Slaying Witness"; "Doug Eller Dies at 56; Former Citizen Reporter," *Asheville Citizen*, March 30, 1960.
305. "Uncle Believes Girl Was Slain by an Intruder," *Asheville Citizen*, July 28, 1936.
306. "Prof. Clevenger, Slaying Witness."
307. Shipp, "Sheriff's Armor-Plated Automobile."
308. "Uncle Believes Girl."
309. Ibid.
310. "Three Men Held in Clevenger Case," *Asheville Citizen*, July 19, 1936; "Bits of News Picked Up in Slaying Probe," *Asheville Citizen*, July 28, 1936; "Officers Study Blood Stains in Clevenger Case," *Asheville Citizen*, July 28, 1936.

311. Ibid.

312. "Uncle Believes Slaying of Girl 'Inside Affair,'" *Asheville Citizen*, July 30, 1936; "Uncle Thinks Niece Murder an Inside Job," *Greenville News*, July 30, 1936.

313. "Uncle Believes Girl."

314. Ibid; "Officers Study Blood Stains."

315. Gudger, Brown and Rudlin, "Rapist Murder"; "Speedy Trial Planned."

316. "Prof. Clevenger, Slaying Witness."

317. "Drunk Boasts of What He Knows 'About Asheville,'" *Asheville Times*, July 27, 1936.

## *Chapter 6*

318. "Wollner's Alibi Witness Held"; "Hotel Pass Key Sheds Light."

319. "Thinks Gaddy Can Provide Solution."

320. Ibid.

321. "False Clues Run Down."

322. Strayer, "Clevenger Murder."

323. "Hotel Pass Key Sheds Light."

324. Ibid; "Fingerprints in Case Studied," *Asheville Citizen*, August 1, 1936; "False Clues Run Down"; "New Attacks Hammer Alibi."

325. "A Proclamation by the Governor," July 20, 1936, Laurence E. Brown Collection, Swannanoa Valley Museum & History Center, Black Mountain, North Carolina; "Letter from Governor John C.B. Ehringhaus to Sheriff Laurence E. Brown," July 23, 1936, Laurence E. Brown Collection, Swannanoa Valley Museum & History Center, Black Mountain, North Carolina.

326. "False Clues Run Down"; "State Summons 31 Witnesses in Clevenger Case," *Asheville Citizen*, August 14, 1936.

327. Gudger, Brown and Rudlin, "Rapist Murder."

328. James Fleming, Buncombe County, North Carolina 1940 U.S. Census, population schedule.

329. Gudger, Brown and Rudlin, "Rapist Murder."

330. Ibid.

331. Ibid.; "Brown Predicts Arrest of Slayer."

332. "Brown Predicts Arrest of Slayer."

333. "City Policeman Is Dismissed, Another Hired," *Asheville Citizen*, April 9, 1948; "James E. Fleming," *Asheville Citizen*, March 21, 1985; "James E. Fleming," death certificate, March 20, 1936.

334. "Thinks Gaddy Can Provide Solution."

335. "Roddey Denies Knowing About Girl's Slaying," *Asheville Citizen*, July 29, 1936.

336. "Thinks Gaddy Can Provide Solution."

337. "Officers Study Blood Stains."

338. Gudger, Brown and Rudlin, "Rapist Murder"; "Clevenger Returns for Questioning."

339. Ibid.; Carl Warren, "Suspicion Turns to Watchman in Co-Ed Killing," *New York Daily News*, July 22, 1936; "Roddey Denies Knowing About Girl's Slaying."

340. "Roddey Denies Knowing About Girl's Slaying."

341. Carl Warren, "Two More Hotel Workers Seized in Co-Ed Killing," *New York Daily News*, July 22, 1936.

342. "Tells of Screams Heard."

343. Ibid.

344. "Seek White in Co-ed Murder," *Philadelphia Tribune*, August 6, 1936.

345. Gudger, Brown and Rudlin, "Rapist Murder."

346. Ibid.

347. Ibid.

348. "Baltimore Newsman Gives Inside Facts on Murder," *Waynesville Mountaineer*, August 6, 1936.

349. Gudger, Brown and Rudlin, "Rapist Murder."

350. "Ex-Police Chief Orr Dies at 74," *Charlotte News*, April 24, 1957; Chuck McShane, "The Story of Charlotte, Part 8: Like the Wild, Wild West," *Charlotte Magazine*, November 18, 2014, https://www.charlottemagazine.com/the-story-of-charlotte-part-8-like-the-wild-wild-west.

351. Gudger, Brown and Rudlin, "Rapist Murder."

352. Ibid.

353. Ibid.

354. Ibid.

355. "Speedy Trial Planned."

356. Brown and Sumner, "Revelations of Mystery and Horror."

357. Gudger, Brown and Rudlin, "Rapist Murder"; Brown and Sumner, "Revelations of Mystery and Horror."

358. Gudger, Brown and Rudlin, "Rapist Murder."

359. Brown and Sumner, "Revelations of Mystery and Horror."

360. Gudger, Brown and Rudlin, "Rapist Murder."

361. "Gaddy and Bell Boys Examined," *Asheville Citizen*, August 7, 1936.

362. "Daniel Gaddy Begins Fourth Week in Jail," *Asheville Citizen*, August 9, 1936.

363. Brown and Sumner, "Revelations of Mystery and Horror."

364. "Daniel Gaddy Begins Fourth Week."

## *Chapter 7*

365. "Sleuth Asked in Co-ed Case," *Charlotte Observer*, August 2, 1936.

366. Letter from Laurence E. Brown to Tauck Tours, July 30, 1936, Laurence Brown Papers, Swannanoa Valley Museum & History Center, Black Mountain, North Carolina; Letter from Laurence E. Brown to Chief of Police, Winchester, Virginia, July 30, 1936, Laurence Brown Papers, Swannanoa Valley Museum & History Center, Black Mountain, North Carolina; Letter from Laurence E. Brown to Chief of Homicide Squad, New York City, New York, July 30, 1936, Laurence Brown Papers, Swannanoa Valley Museum & History Center, Black Mountain, North Carolina.

367. Gudger, Brown and Rudlin, "Rapist Murder."

368. Brown and Sumner, "Revelations of Mystery and Horror."

369. Gudger, Brown and Rudlin, "Rapist Murder."

370. Ibid.

371. Brown and Sumner, "Revelations of Mystery and Horror."

372. Ibid.

373. Ibid.

374. Ibid; "Clevenger Murder Case Is Solved."

375. Gudger, Brown and Rudlin, "Rapist Murder."

376. Brown and Sumner, "Revelations of Mystery and Horror."

377. Ibid.

378. Ibid; Gudger, Brown and Rudlin, "Rapist Murder"; "Clevenger Murder Case Is Solved."

379. "Clevenger Murder Case Is Solved."

380. Ibid.

381. Brown and Sumner, "Revelations of Mystery and Horror."

382. Gudger, Brown and Rudlin, "Rapist Murder."

383. Brown and Sumner, "Revelations of Mystery and Horror."

384. Ibid.

385. Ibid.

386. Ibid.

387. Ibid; Gudger, Brown and Rudlin, "Rapist Murder"; "Clevenger Murder Case Is Solved."

388. Gudger, Brown and Rudlin, "Rapist Murder."

389. Ibid.

390. Ibid.

391. Brown and Sumner, "Revelations of Mystery and Horror."

392. Gudger, Brown and Rudlin, "Rapist Murder."

393. Ibid.

394. Ibid.

395. "Clevenger Murder Case Is Solved."

396. Brown and Sumner, "Revelations of Mystery and Horror."

397. "Clevenger Murder Case Is Solved."

398. Gudger, Brown and Rudlin, "Rapist Murder."

399. Ibid.

400. Brown and Sumner, "Revelations of Mystery and Horror."

401. Gudger, Brown and Rudlin, "Rapist Murder."

## *Chapter 8*

402. "Fannie Moore," North Carolina, WPA Slave Narratives, Volume XI, Part II.

403. Henry Louis Gates Jr., "How Do I Find Slaves Living on a Plantation During the Revolutionary War?" *The Root*, March 13, 2015. https://www.theroot.com/how-do-i-find-slaves-living-on-a-plantation-during-the-1790859094.

404. Cecley Moore, Spartanburg County, South Carolina, 1900 U.S. Census, population schedule; Oley Moore, Spartanburg County, South Carolina, 1910 U.S. Census, population schedule; Celie Moore, Spartanburg County, South Carolina, 1920 U.S. Census, population schedule.

405. Napolean Moore, Spartanburg County, South Carolina, 1920 U.S. Census, population schedule; Celie Moore, Spartanburg County, South Carolina, 1920 U.S. Census.

406. Napolean Moore, Richmond County, Virginia, 1930 U.S. Census, population schedule.

407. Celie Moore, Buncombe County, North Carolina, 1930 U.S. Census, population schedule.

408. "Re-Enactment of Slaying Recorded by Stenographer," *Asheville Citizen*, August 10, 1936.

409. Celie Moore, Buncombe County, North Carolina, 1930 U.S. Census, population schedule.

410. Ibid.; Celie Moore and Martin Moore, Asheville City Directory, 1935; Moore, Celie and Martin Moore, Asheville City Directory, 1936.

411. Celie Moore, Buncombe County, North Carolina, 1930 U.S. Census, population schedule; Celie Moore and Martin Moore, Asheville City Directory, 1935; Celie Moore and Martin Moore, Asheville City Directory, 1936.

412. "Statement of Martin Moore, Made in Room 509, County Court House, Asheville, N.C.," August 9, 1936, D.H. Ramsey Library, Special Collections, University of North Carolina at Asheville; "Here Is Full Text of Confession of Negro," *Asheville Citizen*, August 10, 1936.

413. "Re-Enactment of Slaying Recorded"; "Speedy Trial Planned."

414. "Re-Enactment of Slaying Recorded."

415. "Speedy Trial Planned."

416. "Re-Enactment of Slaying Recorded."

417. "Light Was Burning in Room When Girl Died," *Asheville Citizen*, July 28, 1936; "Few Tangible Clues Left."

418. "Re-Enactment of Slaying Recorded."

419. "Light Was Burning in Room"; "Few Tangible Clues Left."

420. "Re-Enactment of Slaying Recorded."

421. "Speedy Trial Planned."

422. "Re-Enactment of Slaying Recorded."

423. Ibid.

424. "Speedy Trial Planned."

425. "Re-Enactment of Slaying Recorded."

## *Chapter 9*

426. "Negro Arrested for Clevenger Murder; Confesses to Slaying," *Asheville Citizen-Times*, August 9, 1936.

427. James M. Rogers, "Bring in Your News," *Asheville Citizen*, October 3, 1937.

428. "25,000 Copies of Murder Case Extra Are Sold," *Asheville Citizen*, August 10, 1936.

429. "Girl's Mother Is Elated Over News of Arrest," *Asheville Citizen*, August 10, 1936.

430. "Arrest of 'Slayer,'" *Atlanta Daily World*, August 10, 1936.

431. Gamewell Valentine, "Highlights in the News," *Atlanta Daily World*, August 11, 1936.

432. "Under the Microscope," *Philadelphia Tribune*, August 20, 1936.

433. "Local Officers Win Praise for Solving Crime," *Asheville Citizen*, August 11, 1936.

434. Ibid.; "Clevenger Murder Case Is Solved."

435. "Speedy Trial Planned."

436. "London Paper Phones Brown About Arrest," *Asheville Citizen*, August 11, 1936.

437. "Didn't Mean to Kill, Moore Says in Cell," *Charlotte Observer*, August 10, 1936.

438. Telegram from Mr. and Mrs. W.T. Sanderline and Dorothy to Sheriff Lawrence E. Brown, Asheville, Postal Telegraph, August 10, 1936; Telegram from Louis Azrael to Sheriff Laurence H. Brown, Asheville, Western Union, August 10, 1936; Telegram from Bruce Poole, Captain of Detectives, Raleigh Police Department to Sheriff Brown, Asheville Police Dept, Western Union, August 10, 1936; Telegram from A.H. Burnette to Lawrence E. Brown, Sheriff Personal Buncombe Co Asheville, Western Union, August 12, 1936, Laurence Brown Collection, Swannanoa Valley Museum & History Center, Black Mountain.

439. "Local Officers Win Praise."

440. "Plea of Insanity Looms for Confessed Slayer of Young Helen Clevenger," *Asheville Citizen*, August 12, 1936.

441. Ibid.

442. "Speedy Trial Planned."

443. "Plea of Insanity Looms."

444. "Clevenger Murder Case Is Solved."

445. "Didn't Mean to Kill, Moore Says."

446. Ibid.

447. Ibid.

448. Ibid.

449. "Clevenger Murder Case Is Solved"; "Speedy Trial Planned."

450. "Pleads Not Guilty," *Zebulon Record*, August 21, 1936.

451. "Speedy Trial Planned."

452. Ibid.

453. "State Summons 31 Witnesses."

454. "Plea of Insanity Looms."

455. Ibid.

456. "Speedy Trial Planned."

457. "Negro Will Die on Gallows at Sunrise Today," *Asheville Citizen*, August 14, 1936; "1,000 See Negro Pay for Crime," *Asheville Citizen*, August 16,

1936; "Rainey Bethea Dies on Gallows; Trap Sprung by Ex-Louisville Cop," *Owensboro (KY) Messenger*, August 14, 1936.

458. "Plea of Insanity Looms"; "Stage Set for Trial of Martin Moore for Young Girl's Murder," *Asheville Times*, August 18, 1936.

459. Ibid.

460. "Here's One Man Who Is Certain to Attend Trial," *Asheville Citizen*, August 19, 1936; "State v. Martin Moore. August 17, 1936."

461. "Preparations Are Made for Moore's Trial," *Asheville Citizen*, August 16, 1936.

462. "Moore Arraigned on Murder Count in Co-Ed Slaying," *Asheville Citizen*, August 18, 1936; "State v. Martin Moore. August 17, 1936."

463. "Moore Arraigned on Murder Count."

464. "Old Law Ritual Starts Co-Ed Slayer to Gas," *New York Daily News*, August 18, 1936.

465. "Plea of Insanity Looms"; "Moore Arraigned on Murder Count."

466. "Old Law Ritual Starts Co-Ed Slayer to Gas."

467. History.com Editors, "Scottsboro Boys," History, A&E Television Networks, February 22, 2018, https://www.history.com/topics/great-depression/scottsboro-boys.

468. "Moore Arraigned on Murder Count"; "Old Law Ritual Starts Co-Ed Slayer to Gas."

469. "State v. Martin Moore. August 17, 1936."

470. "Moore Goes on Trial Today in Clevenger Case," *Asheville Citizen*, August 19, 1936.

471. "State Begins Testimony."

472. Ibid.; NCDCR archives, copy of note from Dr. L.O. Miller, August 19, 1936.

473. "Negro Charged with Perjury," *Asheville Citizen*, July 1, 1939; "Gets Suspended Sentence for Jury Service," *Carolina Times*, April 27, 1940.

474. "State Begins Testimony."

475. Ibid.

476. "State Begins Testimony"; "Eight Examined as Moore Trial Opens," *Roxboro Courier*, August 20, 1936.

477. "State Begins Testimony."

478. "Eight Examined as Moore Trial Opens."

479. H.G. Trotter, "Witness Tell of Finding Helen's Body," *Charlotte Observer*, August 20, 1936.

480. "State Begins Testimony."

481. Ibid.

482. "State's Witnesses Link Moore"; "Father of Clevenger Girl Faints at Trial," *Asheville Citizen*, August 21, 1936; "Two Witnesses Tell About Moore Confessing Clevenger Slaying," *Asheville Citizen*, August 21, 1936.

483. "State Begins Testimony."

484. "State's Witnesses Link Moore"; "Two Witnesses Tell About Moore Confessing."

485. "State Begins Testimony."

486. Ibid.

487. Ibid.

488. Staley A. Cook, "Asheville Wary of Talk as Slayer of Helen Clevenger Goes on Trial," *Daily Times-News* (Burlington, NC), August 20, 1936.

489. "Sidelights on Trial of Clevenger Case," *Asheville Citizen*, August 21, 1936.

490. Ibid.

491. "State's Witnesses Link Moore."

492. Ibid.

493. Ibid.

494. "Two Witnesses Tell About Moore Confessing"; "N.Y. Experts Link Moore's Gun."

495. "Denies Moore Bought Pistol at Pawn Shop," *Asheville Citizen*, August 11, 1936; "State's Witnesses Link Moore"; "Two Witnesses Tell About Moore Confessing."

496. "State's Witnesses Link Moore."

497. Brian Heard, *Forensic Ballistics in Court: Interpretation and Presentation of Firearms Evidence* (N.p.: John Wiley & Sons, 2013), 33–42.

498. "Baffling Clevenger Murder Case Solved by One Simple Clue," *Asheville Citizen*, August 10, 1936.

499. "N.Y. Experts Link Moore's Gun."

500. "State's Witnesses Link Moore."

501. Ibid.

502. "N.Y. Experts Link Moore's Gun."

503. Ibid.; "State's Witnesses Link Moore"; "Chemistry Links Moore to Crime," *Asheville Times*, August 11, 1936.

504. "N.Y. Experts Link Moore's Gun."

505. Ibid.; "State's Witnesses Link Moore."

506. "N.Y. Experts Link Moore's Gun."

507. Ibid.

508. Ibid.

509. "State's Witnesses Link Moore."

510. Ibid.

511. "State's Witnesses Link Moore"; "Negro Arrested for Clevenger Murder."

512. Ibid.; "N.Y. Experts Link Moore's Gun."

513. "N.Y. Experts Link Moore's Gun."

514. "Murder Case Expected to Go to Jury Today," *Asheville Citizen*, August 22, 1936.

## *Chapter 10*

515. "Sidelights on Trial of Clevenger Case"; "Murder Case Expected to Go to Jury Today."

516. "Father of Clevenger Girl Faints."

517. "Sidelights on Trial of Clevenger Case."

518. Ibid.

519. "Father of Clevenger Girl Faints."

520. "Moore Declares He 'Confessed' Murder after Officers Beat Him," *Asheville Citizen*, August 22, 1936.

521. Ibid.

522. "Praised by Valentine; Detectives Commended for Solving Clevenger Murder Case," *New York Times*, August 14, 1936.

523. Ethelred Brown, "Letters from Readers to the Editor: Great Detective Work?" *New York Amsterdam News*, August 29, 1936.

524. Edwin Grimsley, African American Wrongful Convictions Throughout History, Innocence Project, February 28, 2013.

525. Richard Wright, "How 'Bigger' Was Born," in *A Turbulent Voyage: Readings in African American Studies*, ed. Floyd Windom Hayes III (San Diego: Collegiate Press, 2000), 218–35.

526. Ernest Lindley, "Now They're Praising Hugo Black," Congressional Record, Proceedings and Debates of the 76th Congress Third Session, Appendix, Vol. 86, Part 13, January 3, 1940 to March 5, 1940, United States Government Printing Office; "Mr. Justice Black, Extension of Remarks of Hon. George W. Norris of Nebraska in the Senate of the United States," February 26, 1940. [From Labor of February 20, 1940.]

527. "Moore Declares He 'Confessed' Murder After Officers Beat Him."

528. "Two Witnesses Tell About Moore Confessing"; "Murder Case Expected to Go to Jury Today."

529. "Murder Case Expected to Go to Jury Today."
530. "Moore Declares He 'Confessed' Murder After Officers Beat Him."
531. Ibid.
532. "Murder Case Expected to Go to Jury Today."
533. "Moore Declares He 'Confessed' Murder After Officers Beat Him."
534. "Murder Case Expected to Go to Jury Today."
535. Ibid.
536. "Moore Declares He 'Confessed' Murder After Officers Beat Him";
    "Moore Offers Alibi for Night of Murder," *Charlotte Observer*, August 22, 1936.
537. Ibid.
538. "Murder Case Expected to Go to Jury Today."
539. Ibid.
540. "Confessed Slayer of Girl Examined by Two Alienists," *Asheville Citizen*,
    August 13, 1936.
541. Affidavit and Petition from J. Scroop Styles, August 13, 1936; The order
    from the judge on August 14, 1936, in State Archives of North Carolina,
    Buncombe County Criminal Actions, *State v. Martin Moore*.
542. "Murder Case Expected to Go to Jury Today."
543. Trotter, "Moore Offers Alibi for Night of Murder"; "Murder Case
    Expected to Go to Jury Today."
544. "Moore to Die for Clevenger Murder," *Asheville Citizen*, August 23, 1936.
545. Ibid.
546. "Co-Ed Murder Goes to Jury," Sunday News, *New York Daily News*,
    August 23, 1936.
547. Ibid.
548. "Moore to Die for Clevenger Murder."
549. "Co-Ed Murder Goes to Jury."
550. "Moore to Die for Clevenger Murder."
551. Ibid.
552. Ibid.
553. "Sidelights of Clevenger Trial," *Asheville Citizen*, August 23, 1936.
554. "Martin Moore Is Convicted," *Franklin Times* (Louisburg, NC), August
    28, 1936.
555. "Moore to Die for Clevenger Murder."
556. Ibid.
557. "Martin Moore Is Convicted."
558. "Moore Is Placed on Death Row in State Prison," *Asheville Citizen*,
    August 23, 1936; "Moore Admits Slaying to Prison Officials," *Asheville
    Citizen*, August 24, 1936.

559. "Moore Admits Slaying to Prison Officials"; "Family Drops Fight to Save Martin Moore," *Asheville Citizen*, August 25, 1936.

## *Chapter 11*

560. "Martin Moore's Mother Believes Son Is Innocent," *Asheville Citizen*, August 24, 1936.

561. "Family Drops Fight to Save Martin Moore."

562. "Guilt of Convicted Bell Boy Is Doubted," *Pittsburgh Courier*, September 19, 1936.

563. "Negroes to Meet Today to Discuss Moore Case," *Asheville Citizen*, August 23, 1936; "Negroes Vote to Aid Moore in His Appeal," *Asheville Citizen*, August 24, 1936.

564. "Guilt of Convicted Bell Boy Is Doubted."

565. "The Law Takes Its Course," *Asheville Citizen*, August 23, 1936.

566. "In the Wake of the Asheville Trial," *Franklin Times* (Louisburg, NC), August 28, 1936.

567. "Negro Wounded; Assailant Held," *Asheville Citizen*, August 30, 1936; "Murder Trial of Negro Here Is Nearing Close," *Asheville Citizen*, September 24, 1936.

568. "Moore Admits Slaying to Prison Officials."

569. Ibid.

570. "Bell Boy Hints He 'Will Talk'—Protests Innocence," *Pittsburgh Courier*, August 29, 1936.

571. "Moore Confesses Clevenger Murder to State Officials," *Asheville Citizen*, August 27, 1936.

572. Ibid.

573. "Confession of Martin Moore to Edwin Gill, Commissioner of Paroles," August 26, 1936, Lawrence Brown Collection, Swannanoa Valley Museum & History Center, Black Mountain, North Carolina.

574. "The Stay of Execution," *Statesville (NC) Daily Record*, October 9, 1936.

575. "Appeal of Moore Is Ruled Out," *Asheville Citizen*, October 27, 1936.

576. "Counsel Makes Move to Save Martin Moore," *Asheville Citizen*, November 18, 1936.

577. "Court Rules Moore Must Die for Crime," *Charlotte Observer*, November 26, 1936; "Negro Slayer of Co-Ed Loses Appeal to Court," *Raleigh News and Observer*, November 26, 1936.

578. "'Going to Heaven,'" *Raleigh News and Observer*, December 8, 1936.

579. "Innocent Man Facing Death, Gill Is Told," *Raleigh News and Observer*, December 9, 1936; "Reprieve for Moore Is Sought," *Asheville Citizen*, December 9, 1936.

580. Ibid.

581. Ibid.

582. Ibid; "Negro Slayer of Co-Ed Loses Appeal"; "No Mercy Ahead for Co-Ed Killer," *Raleigh News and Observer*, December 3, 1936; "Martin Moore Ready to Die by Gas Friday," *Charlotte News*, December 7, 1936.

583. John A. Parris Jr., "Moore Spends Last Sunday on Death Row," *Times-News* (Hendersonville, NC), December 7, 1936.

584. Ibid.

585. Ibid.

586. "Martin Moore Ready to Die by Gas."

587. "Moore Baptized; Will Die Friday," *Times-News* (Hendersonville, NC), December 10, 1936; A.T. Dill Jr., "Moore, as Hope Ebbs, Is Baptized at Prison," *Raleigh News and Observer*, December 10, 1936.

588. "Negro Slayer of Co-Ed Loses Appeal"; "No Mercy Ahead for Co-Ed Killer"; "Martin Moore Ready to Die by Gas"; "Plea Is Denied by Ehringhaus," *Charlotte Observer*, December 10, 1936.

589. Dill, "Moore, as Hope Ebbs, Is Baptized"; "2,000 Wanted to Witness Moore's Execution," *Raleigh News and Observer*, December 11, 1936.

590. Letter from H.H. Honeycutt to Lawrence Brown, December 7, 1936, Lawrence Brown Collection, Swannanoa Valley Museum & History Center, Black Mountain, North Carolina.

591. "2,000 Wanted to Witness."

592. Ibid.

593. "Clevenger Killer Dies," *Charlotte News*, December 11, 1936; "Cyanide Death Closes Sensational Murder Case," *Raleigh News and Observer*, December 12, 1936.

594. "Martin Moore Put to Death in Gas Room," *Charlotte News*, December 11, 1936.

595. "N.Y. Co-ed's Murderer Dies in Gas Chamber," *New York Daily News*, December 12, 1936.

596. "Cyanide Death Closes Sensational Murder Case."

597. "Martin Moore Dies in State Gas Chamber," *Asheville Citizen*, December 12, 1936.

598. Ibid.

599. Ibid.

600. Ibid.; John A. Parris Jr., "Lethal Gas Execution of Negro Who Killed Co-Ed Is Described," *Knoxville Journal*, December 12, 1936.

601. "Views and Observations," *Raleigh News and Observer*, December 12, 1936; "Lethal Gas Execution of Negro."

602. "Views and Observations"; "Cyanide Death Closes Sensational Murder Case"; "Lethal Gas Execution of Negro."

## *Chapter 12*

603. William Pickens, "Was Martin Moore Guilty of Hotel Murder? Read This If You Think He Was!" *Atlanta Daily World*, December 20, 1936; William Pickens, "'Politics'—Pickens Tells 'Inside Story' Of Co-Ed 'Slayer' Death 'Murder,'" *Philadelphia Tribune*, December 24, 1936; William Pickens, "God! What a World: The Clevenger Case," *New Journal and Guide*, December 26, 1936.

604. Ibid.

605. Ibid.

606. "Prof. Clevenger, Slaying Witness, Leaves Jail."

607. "Did Innocent Man Die for Hotel Crime?" *Pittsburgh Courier*, January 23, 1937.

608. Booker T. Sherrill, Oral History.

609. Henry Robinson, "A Grand and Glorious Feeling," *Asheville Citizen-Times*, August 25, 1985.

610. Sherrill, Oral History.

611. Eugene Rankin Branch, Registration Card, September 12, 1918; Eugene R. Branch, North Carolina, World War I Service Cards, 1917–1919; "Margo Terrace Register Shut," *Asheville Citizen*, December 2, 1928.

612. "Mr. Eugene Branch Weds Miss Dunn, of New Jersey," *Asheville Citizen*, April 25, 1925; Eugene Rankin Branch, Registration Card, September 12, 1918; "Around the Links," *Asheville Citizen*, September 10, 1921; "Rankin-Branch, Marriage Sunday at Mountain Park, Hot Springs," *Asheville Citizen*, July 25, 1898.

613. "Social and Personal," *Asheville Citizen*, November 23, 1919; "Social and Personal," *Asheville Citizen*, December 14, 1919; "Social and Personal," *Asheville Citizen*, December 18, 1919; "Social and Personal," *Asheville Citizen*, August 29, 1920; "Social and Personal," *Asheville Citizen*, September 10, 1920; "News and Activities of Asheville's Social Realm," *Asheville Citizen*,

October 16, 1921; "Dance Is Enjoyed at Asheville Country Club," *Asheville Citizen*, May 19, 1923.

614. "Miss J.J. Wright Weds Patrick H. Branch, Jr.," *Asheville Citizen*, June 22, 1937; Grace R. Branch, Buncombe County, North Carolina, 1930 U.S. Census, population schedule.

615. "Mr. Eugene Branch Weds Miss Dunn."

616. "Many Hotels and Inns Have Served Public in This Popular Mountain Resort Region," *Asheville-Citizen Times*, March 26, 1950.

617. "Margo Terrace Will Be Closed by Estate Dec. 1," *Asheville Citizen*, November 18, 1928.

618. Ibid.

619. "Margo Terrace Register Shut"; "Eugene R Branch Heads Va. Hotel," *Asheville Citizen*, December 6, 1928.

620. "Mrs. Eugene R. Branch," *Richmond Times-Dispatch*, August 15, 1933.

621. Ibid.; "Katherine C. Dunn Branch," death certificate, August 13, 1933.

622. "Engagements Announced in Many Sections, Branch-McDonald," *Richmond Times-Dispatch*, July 14, 1935.

623. "Miss J.J. Wright Weds Patrick H. Branch, Jr"; "Hough Is Named an Executive in Insurance Firm," *Asheville Citizen*, September 12, 1940.

624. Letter from Laurence Brown to Chief of Police, Winchester, VA, July 30, 1936, Laurence Brown Collection, Swannanoa Valley Museum and History Center, Black Mountain, North Carolina.

625. "Speedy Trial Planned."

626. "Girl's Murder Brings Suit Against Battery Park Hotel," *Raleigh News and Observer*, October 16, 1936; "Hotel Sued for Damages After Girl's Slaying," *Tampa Tribune*, October 16, 1936; "Ask $50,000 Damages for Girl's Death," *Asheville Citizen*, October 16, 1936.

627. "Did Innocent Man Die for Hotel Crime?"

628. Appeal by Knott Management Corporation from an order entered by Clement, J., at July Term, 1937, of Buncombe; "Clevenger Damage Suit Rest upon Technicality," *Raleigh News and Observer*, September 10, 1937; "$50,000 Suit Is Withdrawn by Clevenger," *Asheville Citizen*, November 30, 1937.

## *Chapter 13*

629. Sherrill, Oral History; Robinson, "A Grand and Glorious Feeling."

630. Sherrill, Oral History.

631. Lutrelle Wishart, "Art in Asheville," *Asheville Citizen-Times*, April 14, 1963.

632. "Mrs. Essie Ward, Obituary," *Asheville Citizen*, September 13, 1967.

633. "Daniel H. Gaddy Obituary," *Asheville Citizen*, April 5, 1970.

634. "Banks Taylor, Obituary," *Asheville Citizen-Times*, September 20, 1970; Sherrill, Oral History.

635. "L.D. Roddy," *Asheville Citizen*, March 21, 1963; "L.D. Roddy," *Asheville Citizen*, March 23, 1963.

636. "Clevenger Dies at Age of 69," *Asheville Citizen*, June 9, 1951; "Dairy Savant Dies in Sleep," *Charlotte Observer*, June 9, 1951; "W.L. Clevenger," *Chattanooga Daily Times*, June 9, 1951.

637. "Mary Clevenger Rites on Friday," *Piqua Daily Call*, January 28, 1943; "Joseph Clevenger Dies Unexpectedly at Washington, D.C.," *Piqua Daily Call*, July 12, 1945.

638. "Orr Declares Sheriff Brown Retained Him," *Charlotte News*, August 30, 1936.

639. "Walter Orr Is Claiming Clevenger Case Reward," *Charlotte News*, August 27, 1936; "Orr Declares Sheriff Brown Retained Him," *Charlotte News*, August 30, 1936.

640. "New York Detective Disagrees with Orr," *Charlotte News*, August 27, 1936.

641. "Walter Orr Is Claiming Clevenger Case Reward"; "New York Detective Disagrees with Orr"; "Last Year's Headlines," *Charlotte News*, August 27, 1937.

642. "Ace Detective Dies in N.Y.," *Charlotte Observer*, July 14, 1936.

643. "Thomas J. Martin Dies; Former Ace Detective," *Brooklyn Daily Eagle*, December 19, 1945.

644. "Ace Detective Dies in N.Y."; "Thomas J. Martin Dies."

645. "Nettles, Ex-Jurist, Dies at 82," *Asheville Citizen-Times*, March 20, 1976.

646. "Scroop Styles Dies; Noted WNC Attorney," *Asheville Citizen-Times*, April 9, 1967.

647. Lewis Green, *Of Human Interest* (N.p.: iUniverse, 2003).

648. Ibid.

649. Interview with Jake Robertson.

650. "Laurence E. Brown Dies."

651. "Tom Brown Announces for Sheriff," *Asheville Citizen-Times*, January 30, 1970.

652. Interview with Joan Brown and William Brown, Black Mountain, North Carolina, by Anne Chesky Smith, December 13, 2016, Swannanoa Valley Museum and History Center Oral History Collection.

653. Pat H. Branch, Buncombe County, North Carolina, 1920 U.S. Census, population schedule; Pat H. Branch, Buncombe County, North Carolina, 1930 U.S. Census, population schedule; Pat H. Branch, Buncombe County, North Carolina, 1940 U.S. Census, population schedule; "Pat Branch, Hotelman, Is Dead."

654. "Miss J.J. Wright Weds Patrick H. Branch, Jr."; "Hough Is Named an Executive."

655. Asheville City Directory, 1937, 1940, 1947, 1951; Celie, Moore, Buncombe County, North Carolina, 1940 U.S. Census, population schedule.

656. "Battery Park Hotel," National Register of Historic Places.

657. "Martin Moore's Body," *Raleigh News and Observer*, December 16, 1936; "Slayer's Body Goes to Medical Students," *Courier Post*, December 16, 1936.

658. "Med Students Will Carve on Body Martin Moore," *Wake Forest Alumni News* 9, no. 2 (December 1936).

659. Email communication with Ed Morris, executive director, Wake Forest Historical Museum, September 22, 2020.

660. Bob Lynch, "Were They Cadavers?" *News and Observer* (Raleigh, NC), April 15, 1966; "Old Bones Are Human," *News and Observer* (Raleigh, NC), April 16, 1966; "Dr. Mackie Has Devoted Nearly 30 Years of Service to Wake Forest Area," *Wake Weekly* (Wake Forest, NC), January 30, 1959; Bob Lynch, "Old Bones Found in Wake Forest," *News and Observer* (Raleigh, NC), September 24, 1970; "Bruce Thompson Heads List of Talented Colored Folk," *Old Gold and Black*, February 27, 1937.

# INDEX